We Can Teach That

We Can Teach That

Information Literacy for School Librarians

Edited by Ewa Dziedzic-Elliott

ROWMAN & LITTLEFIELD
Lanham • Boulder • New York • London

Published by Rowman & Littlefield
An imprint of The Rowman & Littlefield Publishing Group, Inc.
4501 Forbes Boulevard, Suite 200, Lanham, Maryland 20706
www.rowman.com

86-90 Paul Street, London EC2A 4NE

British Library Cataloguing in Publication Information Available

Library of Congress Cataloging-in-Publication Data

Names: Dziedzic-Elliott, Ewa, 1980- editor.

Title: We can teach that: information literacy for school librarians / edited by Ewa Dziedzic-Elliott.
Description: Lanham: Rowman & Littlefield, 2024. | Includes bibliographical references and index. | Summary: "In the academic, education and library worlds we have been using the term information literacy to cover a very broad spectrum of different types of literacies. And here is the most interesting thing: school librarians have been teaching these literacies forever under the terms of library skills and research skills"– Provided by publisher.
Identifiers: LCCN 2024033989 (print) | LCCN 2024033990 (ebook) | ISBN 9781538189085 (cloth) | ISBN 9781538189092 (paperback) | ISBN 9781538189108 (ebook)
Subjects: LCSH: Information literacy–Study and teaching–United States. | School libraries–United States. | School librarian participation in curriculum planning–United States. | LCGFT: Essays.
Classification: LCC ZA3088.5.S34 W4 2024 (print) | LCC ZA3088.5.S34 (ebook) | DDC 027.80973-dc23/eng/20240819
LC record available at https://lccn.loc.gov/2024033989
LC ebook record available at https://lccn.loc.gov/2024033990

♾️™ The paper used in this publication meets the minimum requirements of American National Standard for Information Sciences—Permanence of Paper for Printed Library Materials, ANSI/NISO Z39.48-1992.

*To my mom, Halina Dziedzic, my first librarian. I still can close
my eyes and see you in the middle of the night, wrapped up
in a warm sweater with a book on your lap, reading.
To my family, my wonderful children, Katie, Lizzie, and Jan, and my
husband, Mark, who stand by me when I disappear into the abyss of the
library world. I could have never done what I do without your support.
Thank you!*

Contents

Foreword

Information is known as the stock-in-trade for librarians, but its characteristics, delivery formats, and context seem to change continually. In trying to keep up, school librarians can easily find themselves in Lewis Carroll's world: "My dear, here we must **run as fast as** we can, just to stay in place. And if you wish to **go** anywhere you must **run** twice **as fast as that**" (*Alice in Wonderland*).

But all is not lost. The positive stance, foundational ideas, and practical strategies in this collection of articles by leading school librarians and educators will inspire, challenge, and guide a rethinking process about the school librarian's role in teaching essential information literacy skills and strategies. Librarians are encouraged to think about their "Why?" as the foundation for their library programs. Why is information literacy so important for our learners? The answer is clear. Information literacy empowers our young people with the attitudes and skills to take charge of their own futures.

The concept of information literacy is broadly defined to include multiple literacies within its umbrella: information, media, tech, visual, health, cultural and multilingual, and financial. Our learners are surrounded by information presented in multiple formats; the charge to librarians is to ensure that students develop the ability to extract valid information from whatever format is most appropriate for their information needs.

Once librarians have solidified their vision on the scope and importance of information literacy, they must begin the hard work of recognizing the implications of the technology-driven and constantly changing context for teaching and learning. Information is being shaped by the format in which it is delivered; learners must be taught the critical skepticism needed to use search engines, databases, websites, print materials, and social media thoughtfully and to recognize the impact of the presentation format on their own emotions and understandings. Librarians do not have to be experts on Instagram or TikTok, but they do have to identify and teach learners to apply critical thinking and evaluation lenses to their use.

The information-literacy skills that learners need cannot be taught in one-time, scattershot lessons. They need to be developed and practiced over the years of schooling in a continuum of experiences and lessons. Librarians with learners at every grade level, from primary through high school, will find practical strategies and lesson ideas in this book. Librarians will be able to recognize the value of introducing information-literacy concepts to the youngest learners and then teaching more complex skills as they progress through the grades so that learners develop critical thinking skills and information-literacy habits of mind. Librarians can develop an articulated curriculum for their school that meets the priorities of the school administration and teachers and enables learners to hone their information-literacy skills.

School librarians do not bear the sole responsibility for integrating these essential learning skills into content learning across the school. By collaborating with classroom teachers, librarians can integrate the teaching of durable information skills within the context of different subject areas. Classroom teachers discover that students learn content more deeply when they employ skills to make learning choices and draw meaning for themselves. Librarians are pleasantly surprised that students learn to transfer their skills to multiple learning situations.

Practicing librarians are not the only voices heard in this collection. Featured in a separate chapter are non-school library education and information specialists, including academic librarians, library supervisors, and library educators. Their contributions feature comparisons between the standards of the American Association of School Librarians and the Association of College and Research Libraries, the value of partnerships between academic and school librarians, a new model for evaluating school librarians, the national perspective on information literacy, and a library educator's emphasis on the power of teaching visual literacy. Their perspectives add both depth and context to the practical articles and enable school library professionals to recognize their affinity with other librarians and information professionals.

Throughout the book, school librarians are urged, both implicitly and explicitly, to become leaders of positive change in their schools. The rationale and context for teaching information literacy are complemented by practical examples and strategies offered by librarians with learners from the primary grades to high school. The message from the book for the school library profession is that we need to seize every opportunity to empower all our learners with the life skills of information literacy. And we **can** do that!

Barbara Stripling, professor emerita, School of Information Studies, Syracuse University, New York

Preface

Ewa Dziedzic-Elliott

Information Literacy (IL) has garnered much attention as more states consider following the New Jersey legislature in passing an information literacy student learning standards bill.[1] The New Jersey bill describes the current working definition of K–12 information literacy as follows:

C.18A:7F-4.4 New Jersey Student Learning Standards, information literacy; definition.

1. a. As used in this act, the term "information literacy" means a set of skills that enables an individual to recognize when information is needed and to locate, evaluate, and use effectively the needed information. Information literacy includes, but is not limited to, digital, visual, media, textual, and technological literacy.
    b. The State Board of Education shall adopt New Jersey Student Learning Standards in information literacy. The content of information literacy shall include, at a minimum:
        (1) the research process and how information is created and produced;
        (2) critical thinking and using information resources;
        (3) research methods, including the difference between primary and secondary sources;
        (4) the difference between facts, points of view, and opinions;
        (5) accessing peer-reviewed print and digital library resources;
        (6) the economic, legal, and social issues surrounding the use of information; and
        (7) the ethical production of information. [2]

I wanted to start with this definition to point to a couple of aspects of it; for example, the expansion of the typical research skills terminology and the addition of specific terms such as types of literacies under the umbrella of IL: digital, visual, media, textual, and technological literacy. The second part of the legislation outlines the process of creating and producing information, the application of critical thinking skills, and an assessment of it through the lens of academic-level research, the types of received information, and the ability to decode it. What I truly appreciate in this document is the obligation to teach students about being the receivers, producers, and sharers of the information, information's value and credibility, and not being passive observers.

After the passing of the legislation, it became apparent that there were challenges that came with the expectation to teach IL, such as:

- Who is going to teach information literacy (not every Pre-K–12 school library has a certified school librarian that can teach the subject).[3]
- How can we best support Pre-K–12 school librarians in preparation for the new standards?
- How can we support educators who might be asked to teach information literacy if they don't have school library training?
- How can we draw from the expertise of those who already implement information literacy in their daily practice?

I proposed putting together a handbook for school librarians and educators created in collaboration with colleagues from various institutions across the country. I was very humbled to learn that my desire to help others teach information literacy in our schools was accepted.

What you find in front of you is a collection of essays written by practicing Pre-K–12 librarians, academic librarians, and college/university professors who research and teach librarianship and IL.

You will notice that the book has two very distinct writing styles: school librarians lean more on giving specific examples and sharing their best practices, while practicing academic librarians and higher education instructors focus more on literature reviews and lean toward an academic writing style. I find the blend of the two very beneficial as they give us glimpses into their work environments, instruction styles, librarianship realities, and a very deep understanding of various types of information literacy.

I hope that this volume will find its place on the shelves of professional literature collections for Pre-K–12 school librarians and educators, as well as in higher education, especially for students working toward library science and education degrees.

NOTES

1. "Bill Text: NJ S588," Section C.18A:7F-4.4 1b, LegiScan (January 4, 2023), C.18A:7F-4.4 1b, https://legiscan.com/NJ/text/S588/2022.
2. Ibid.
3. See: Slide Study https://libslide.org/.

Ewa Dziedzic-Elliott

Acknowledgments

I would like to thank Erinn Slanina, the editor of Rowman & Littlefield, for her guidance in the process.

I would also like to thank the whole team of librarians from New Jersey, especially from the New Jersey Association of School Librarians, who do not take no for an answer, continue to believe in the core principles of librarianship, and always put students and their well-being first. Thank you for introducing me to the world of a professional organization that not only is capable of taking a state lead in the areas of legislation, advocacy, and student learning needs, but also assists others across the country. I am always in awe of your knowledge, preparedness, passion, and ability to see the bigger picture in building our library ecosystem.

And thank you to my library mentors, especially Joyce K. Valenza and Brenda Boyer, who believed in me, included me in their projects, and encouraged me to explore what this foreign-born, second-generation librarian is capable of presenting in the field of librarianship.

Ewa Dziedzic-Elliott

1

Visual Literacy

Rachel Anne Mencke, Librarian, St. Matthew's Parish School, California

As school librarians, how do we train preschoolers and grade schoolers to think critically about media, information sources, and technology that we cannot imagine yet? Surely, that's a challenge we can push off to the upper grades, right?

On the contrary, it is never too early to lay the groundwork of skills that will allow students to intelligently engage with the shifting media landscape. Even before children can read fluently, they are active and curious interpreters of the world around them. Focusing on visual literacy is an excellent way to start honing children's analytical abilities while maintaining a sense of joyful play. Visual literacy is an area where students can learn and gain confidence in the same skills that they will apply to critically interpret a broad range of media later in life. Illustrations are beautiful, and interpreting them feels easy and fun when the mechanics of reading are still an obstacle to interacting with texts. Engaging with pictures helps to preserve the joy and fun of learning.

With the very youngest children, this is often as simple as taking a "picture book walk" and previewing a book by discussing the illustrations before reading it. What is happening in each illustration? How do you think the characters feel? What do you think is going to happen next? Far from a passively received performance, story time should be a vibrant exchange of ideas and imaginings. Toddlers and preschoolers are kinetic and unfiltered in their reactions to stories. Instead of trying to squelch all the "shouty-outies," embrace the audience participation. If a child shouts, "Oooooh, he's mad!," ask, "How do you know?" If there's a chorus of "Uh-oh!" and "Oh, no!," ask, "Why do you think that's a bad thing?" Sometimes, a three-year-old can be surprisingly insightful in their comment: "I know he's mad 'cause of his eyebrows!" or "Something bad is going to happen because it got all dark and spooky." Often, the youngest listeners will notice details in the illustrations that adults have missed. "Mina's the only one who always has her eyes open," a child pointed out when I read *Mina* by Matthew Forsythe.[1] Inviting and honoring these insights builds children's confidence in their ability to interpret the world around them, which in turn encourages them to apply that skill to more situations.

As grade-schoolers gain reading fluency, there is a tendency for both kids and adults to privilege the written word. I like to draw my students' attention to the ways that all parts of a work function together. When introducing the concept of plot to kindergarteners, I share *One Day, The End: Short, Very Short, Shorter-Than-Ever Stories* by Rebecca Kai Dotlich.[2] Keeping the illustrations hidden, I read the text first: "One day, I went to school. I came home. The end."[3] Not much of a story, right? Then, we examine the illustrations together, and students draw out the complexities. "Do the words tell the whole story, or do you need to slow down and look at the pictures, too?" Together, we compose a fuller retelling of the story, using details from each two-page spread. Later, I challenge students: "Do you think you can tell a story with characters, a setting, and a plot without any words at all?" Many excellent wordless or near-wordless picture books have been published in the last few decades. *Good Dog, Carl!*[4] and *Mr. Wuffles!*[5] are perennial favorites in my library. With slightly older groups, I take a conspiratorial tone. "There's a lot going on here. Do you think an author could describe all that to little kids in words they could understand, or would they have to make the story less complicated?"

In third grade, my school's art teacher, Giuliana Caredda, and I collaborate on a visual storytelling unit. Many of my students are graphic novel-crazy, and we invite them to realize just how complicated comics are. In the first class, we look at examples of different ways that stories can rely on illustrations, from classic wordless picture books like *Journey* by Aaron Becker[6] to books where the pictures entirely change the meaning of the words. I read *My Cat, The Silliest Cat in the World* by Gilles Bachelet,[7] where the humorous conceit is that the author's "cat" is clearly an elephant. Authors can rely entirely on illustrations, use illustrations to complement their words, or even use illustrations to contradict their words entirely. Reading the pictures is key to getting the full story. In our second session, we walk through the first few pages of Molly Bang's *Picture This: How Pictures Work.*[8] The kids are excited to discuss the way that size, shape, and color can express ideas like personality, danger, and vulnerability. "Whoa! It's just a triangle, but it's totally Little Red Riding Hood!" one student said. Afterward, we share an illustrated book and discuss the ways the illustrator used Molly Bang's principles. How does the artist use colors and shape to direct our attention? Can you see the way these jagged lines feel dangerous, or these curves feel cozy? *Mina* lands differently with older readers than with preschoolers and is a wonderful example that plays with the tension when illustrations and text disagree; "It's a squirrel," her father announces when he brings home a cat. Next, we look at the comic format, with a lesson on comic terminology, and a look at some of the storytelling techniques comic artists use. I like to show kids the continuum of realistic-abstract faces in *Understanding Comics* by Scott McCloud.[9] Many of the concepts in this book are over the kids' heads, but they eagerly connect with the idea that simplified, abstract figures are more universal. Moreover, students are empowered by understanding that they don't need to be da Vinci to illustrate a satisfying comic. Instead, the challenge is to find the simplest combination of shapes and colors that can effectively express a character. Dav Pilkey's *Dog Man* series takes the character of Petey through a meaningful redemption arc that is accessible to emerging readers—quite a feat with minimal text and childlike illustrations. The unit culminates in a project where students create their own short comics. Some of the results have eventually been cataloged in our collection and subsequently checked out by a wide range of students and faculty.

Of course, book illustrations are not the only format that students need to be competent at decoding. In second grade, my students learn that media is something that carries a message to lots of people. The analogy I like to use is that media is the speech bubble carrying the message, not the message itself. We spend some time identifying media in our daily environments: the logos on sweatshirts, the ads on radio and TV, video games, podcasts, TikTok videos, YouTube channels, books, websites, songs, and billboards. The mere act of identifying that something is media helps students learn to think critically about what they are absorbing. A wonderful Canadian organization called MediaSmarts provides a free K–2 online lesson plan called *Break the Fake: What's in the Frame?*[10] The lesson, which begins with convincing documentary footage of tiny "house hippos," is fun and accessible for younger students, who learn about one way that videos and images can be manipulated to fool people. The concluding art activity plays into children's love of trickery in a gentle and memorable way. A few weeks later, I follow up with a compilation of toy commercials and Ryan's World-type sponsored videos. "How do you think this is supposed to make kids feel?" "Does anyone have that toy? Does it really do that? Do you think they edited out the parts where it fell over?" Usually, at least one kid volunteers "I got that for Christmas, and it doesn't work like that *at all*," or "I love that game, but it's really only fun if you get a bunch of in-app purchases." While I update the commercial compilation each year, I also intersperse clips from a painfully old Consumer Reports VHS tape called *Buy Me That!*[11] The kids and I laugh about the hairstyles and clothes, but I think it's actually valuable to see how old some advertising tricks are; you don't need CGI or deepfakes to trick people. At the same time, you also don't need forensic technology to suss out untrustworthy messages. Think about what you see! Ask questions!

By mid-elementary grades, visual literacy and verbal literacy start to merge. My fourth graders get a reprise of the House Hippo lesson after we watch the BBC's 1957 Spaghetti Harvest Hoax. (Most school years, at least one braggart claims to have eaten fresh-picked spaghetti.) By this age, we are able to begin working on the idea of lateral reading. Students at around this age are growing from being able to question what they see to learning to verify and cross-check their facts. Common Sense Media's free "Is Seeing Believing?"[12] lesson plan is a great way to remind students that images are frequently changed for a variety of reasons, from entertainment to advertising to April Fools' Day pranks. As a follow-up, I present Meghan McCarthy's amusing nonfiction book *Aliens Are Coming!: The True Account of the 1938 War of the Worlds Radio Broadcast*,[13] and we discuss the reasons why so many people thought the alien invasion was real. "What would you have done differently?" I ask them. The biggest answer is "Turn to a different station and see if it has the same story." "I mean, if the world's getting taken over, someone else is probably going to notice, right?" one child commented.

Whether watching, playing, reading, or listening, kids need to know when they are engaging with media and resist being passive receivers of information. At a time when reading is sometimes daunting, focusing on visual literacy is a fun, playful, and immensely effective way to scaffold children's analytical skills. Students need to recognize that whether they are seeing a logo, watching a video, reading a book, or playing a game, they are engaging with something that was created to carry a message. They need to identify that message and make a conscious decision about how to respond. From infancy, children absorb a wealth of information through their eyes and interpret it without even being aware of the process. When we spark metacognition, students become more aware both of what they are seeing and their power to make sense of it. Hopefully, by the time they are learning to navigate the internet, students are familiar with thinking skeptically about what they see and bringing the same analytical skills to the broad swath of media that informs their lives.

NOTES

1. Matthew Forsythe, *Mina* (Simon & Schuster/Paula Wiseman Books, 2022).
2. Rebecca Kai Dotlich, *One Day ... The End: Short, Very Short, Shorter-Than-Ever Stories* (Boyds Mills Press, 2015).
3. Ibid, 2–3.
4. Alexandra Day, *Good Dog, Carl!* (Little Simon, 1996).
5. David Wiesner, *Mr. Wuffles!* (Clarion Books, 2013).
6. Aaron Becker, *Journey* (Candlewick, 2013).
7. Gilles Bachelet, *My Cat, The Silliest Cat in the World* (Abrams Books for Young Readers, 2006).
8. Molly Bang, *Picture This: How Pictures Work* (Chronicle Books, 2000).
9. Scott McCloud, *Understanding Comics: The Invisible Art* (William Morrow Paperbacks, 1994).
10. "Break the Fake: What's in the Frame? Lesson Plan," MediaSmarts, https://mediasmarts.ca/break-fake-whats-frame.

11. *Buy Me That! A Kids' Survival Guide to TV Advertising*, VHS, directed by Jim Jinkins and Michael Tollin, Consumer Reports, 1989.
12. "Lesson: Is Seeing Believing?," Common Sense Media, last updated August 2018, https://www.commonsense.org/education/digital-citizenship/lesson/is-seeing -believing.
13. Meghan McCarthy, *Aliens Are Coming: The True Account of the 1938 War of the Worlds Radio Broadcast* (Knopf Books for Young Readers, 2006).

2

Navigating Developmental Milestones

INFORMATION LITERACY FOR ELEMENTARY SCHOOL STUDENTS

Amanda Harrison, Assistant Professor of Library Science and Information Services, University of Central Missouri, Missouri

Elementary librarians wishing to teach information literacy to students must remember the wide range of cognitive, social, emotional, and self-awareness stages that students go through during the elementary years. Information literacy is defined by the American Library Association as a set of skills needed by individuals to "recognize when information is needed and have the ability to locate, evaluate, and use effectively the needed information."[1] Librarians must be prepared to help students develop in a wide variety of ways to assist them in finding, learning, evaluating, and retaining information as well as sharing it with others. In many cases, they have to assess students' abilities in performance on traditional skill-based tasks and their ability to self-evaluate, reflect on learning, and put it into practice. A better understanding of the developmental changes occurring in the elementary years can help librarians pinpoint when learning goes awry or develop plans that will be more likely to lead toward success.

COGNITIVE DEVELOPMENT AND EXECUTIVE FUNCTION

Students' cognitive skills develop rapidly as they age, including language development and understanding of abstract concepts. Sherwin and Nielsen note that "A consistent finding in our research over the years is the need to target very narrow age groups when designing for children."[2] For example, even a search engine designed for young children does not apply to every K–6 age group. Instead, Sherwin and Nielsen suggest focusing on age bands 3–5, 6–8, and 9–12.[3]

To be information-literate, an individual needs to be verbally literate. Verbal comprehension is one significant change in cognitive development that children continue to grow and develop throughout their elementary years. Defined verbal comprehension is the ability to understand and communicate with written and spoken words. Written words, or basic literacy skills, are one key feature of information literacy, but communication through the spoken word via increased listening comprehension and vocabulary is also essential. Colognesi notes that listening comprehension is a basis for academic success and can often be predictive of reading success. Even though oral language is innate, teaching listening skills can help ensure that students are listening and comprehending.[4] Verbal comprehension incorporates elements found within fluid intelligence, such as making inferences, forming concepts, recognizing relationships, grasping implications, and transforming data.[5] Visual and relational reasoning are evident in very young children but continue to improve dramatically as children progress to later childhood and adolescence.[6] Students can also be taught aspects of fluid reasoning and intensive instruction has been shown to improve performance, even though the results are variable.[7]

Students' reasoning ability progresses as their understanding moves from concrete to abstract objects throughout elementary school. Students who do not have abstract knowledge will struggle to conduct effective searches, particularly on websites that require an understanding of how objects are classified. Even adults sometimes find websites with deep hierarchical navigation challenging, but website navigation very often confuses children.[8] Some websites designed for children, such as the International Children's Digital Library (ICDL),[9] consider how students wish to browse for information; for example, by including a simultaneous visual search platform that may appear more complex and visually cluttered but is preferred by children.[10]

As students grow and develop, they mature in their executive functioning. This increased maturity impacts their ability to successfully utilize information literacy skills through their increased ability to plan, execute, and evaluate an information search. The Executive Function Mapping Project highlights executive function (EF) as specifically comprising "working memory, response inhibition, attention shifting (also called cognitive flexibility), and attention control." The project also highlights a different set of "regulation-related skills,'" including "self-control, emotion regulation, EF, problem solving, and grit."[11] In particular, Anderson and Johnston consider ways librarians can offer metacognitive strategies or "metastrategies" to assist students through prompting or think-aloud protocols to help students plan, monitor, and evaluate their searches.[12] While their strategies are aimed at college students, similar opportunities written at an appropriate level for younger children could also be utilized. An example of self-prompting at the planning stage might be:

Amanda Harrison

- Planning Prompts
  - What do I need to do to find this information?
  - What is my teacher or librarian asking me to do?
- Monitoring Prompts
  - Do I need help, or do I need to try a different website/database/keyword search?
  - What is hard about this task?
  - What skill can I use to help me?
- Evaluation Prompts
  - Did I learn something new?
  - Did I learn anything unexpected?
  - Am I still wondering about something?

Students who need help with an online search or who need to problem-solve their search strategy often navigate digital sources differently than adults. Sherwin and Nielsen note a wide range of exploratory behaviors in children's use of websites.[13] They found that children want more instant gratification and do not wish to wait for results. However, they also found that children often search for another site if they cannot make the original work as they wish. Furthermore, even when children can read the text online, they often skip over it. These explorations can be beneficial in some scenarios but cause problems in others when librarians note that children skip from site to site, seemingly without absorbing any information. Children need to be prompted to slow down and monitor how their research is going when doing online research in particular.

In addition to metacognitive strategies, students also need visual anchors to help support their use of information sources. Information retrieval systems can be complex, causing memory overload; therefore, children may forget what they have done and the searches they performed.[14,15] Librarians can help students navigate online content by offering visual anchors for students through charts, note-taking, or guided note-taking. King offers another strategy by highlighting ways to teach students to use digital anchors by navigating databases using digital breadcrumbs.[16] This digital anchor helps many young students navigate an online database independently. Written, digital, or visual anchors can be essential: if a student's working memory and cognitive load are taken up entirely by the website design and usability features, they will not be able to take on and learn new content.[17,18]

SOCIAL AND EMOTIONAL LEARNING

Social and emotional development or "regulation-related skills" have seen an increased emphasis in K–12 education in recent years and are an essential part of developing students through the inquiry and information literacy process.

The Committee for Children defines social and emotional learning (SEL) as the "process of developing the self-awareness, self-control, and interpersonal skills that are vital for school, work, and life success."[19] According to *Education Week*, twenty-seven states have SEL competencies as part of their standards for all pre-K through grade 12 students.[20] SEL topics related to inquiry and information literacy include students' ability to be curious, collaborate with others, be self-reflective, take risks in their learning, and be innovative. While there is not yet a research framework that highlights the exact connections between social-emotional maturity and information literacy, some promising studies show a positive relationship between the two.[21,22]

Increased interest in SEL has even contributed to a rise in practical resources for librarians who want to develop student skills in SEL. The 2021 book *Social-Emotional Learning Using Makerspaces and Passion Projects* and SEL-specific activities from Common Sense Media are designed to help students self-reflect and be socially aware while interacting with the digital world and inquiry-based units.[23,24] Indeed, the concept of the Digital Citizen, which is often paired with information literacy instruction, was built on the background of research on young people's development of moral and ethical responsibility online and incorporates lessons that focus on areas of "Self & Personal Well-Being: Dilemmas related to digital footprint, identity, reputational concerns, self-care and well-being."[25]

SCHOOL SKILLS

As students progress through elementary school, they learn and gain skills in many areas that relate to information literacy. Students' growth in reading, digital, media, visual, and other literacy, as well as evaluative skills, helps them contextualize the information they learn. Library programs that teach, enhance, and collaborate on skill-based and literacy-based instruction are setting the foundation for students to be information-literate.

Students start their education years with little to no literacy ability, at least in terms of their ability to search print resources. Yet, according to the Nation's Report Card, 2022 reading scores were lower for students of all levels compared to pre-pandemic averages.[26] Basic reading literacy must still be considered when designing education for elementary children. However, as Biancarosa and Griffiths note, children with reading challenges can still participate in inquiry projects using targeted online resources, especially those with multimedia or read-aloud capabilities.[27]

However, it is not enough simply to have multimedia or adaptive programs available to students. Students must be taught how to use these resources and gain knowledge from them. Even though the concept of the digital native has since been debunked, repeated studies have shown that "the best predictor of how children use websites is how much online practice they have."[28] However, many children's familiarity with digital devices is limited to the games and apps that students use on personal phones and tablets, and this "locked down" interactivity is not always equivalent to the desktop or laptop computers, which are more often used to search for information. More recent studies of children's screen time highlight the ubiquity of smaller phone and tablet devices in most children's homes.[29] Indeed, LaGarde and Hudgins note in their book *Fact Vs Fiction: Teaching Critical Thinking Skills in the Age of Fake News*, that it is vital to teach students how to search and evaluate information on phones and tablets since they frequently use those mediums in their personal lives.[30]

Assessing information and the complete information search process are crucial skills that should be integrated into the information literacy curriculum. Students need help determining the basis for evaluating information and, due to their lack of knowledge and context about many school-related topics, may struggle in stand-alone evaluative lessons. Several models can help students evaluate materials. One, the Currency, Relevance, Authority, Accuracy, and Purpose (CRAAP) Test, exemplifies the stand-alone model of testing research. The model highlights important features of information literacy for older students. However, younger students struggle with many features of evaluating texts as well as the terminology behind them. Furthermore, the CRAAP Test has very specific drawbacks as it doesn't suggest evaluating an information source based on one's question. Nor does it consider how the information source relates to the wider body of knowledge about the topic. Lateral reading, a new concept in information literacy, offers students a better chance to compare and evaluate information sources against one another.[31]

STUDENT RESEARCH MODELS AND FRAMEWORKS

Many librarians teach planning, monitoring, and evaluating information literacy through a structured inquiry model designed to provide students with a view of the process for an extended information search. Several inquiry models consider the role of students' SEL development and their emotional and affective state as it relates to learning. Kuhlthau's information search process was pivotal in determining effective ways to move through the inquiry process. Originally researched with high school students, the information search process developed into the Guided Inquiry Model, which outlines the steps students take during an inquiry assignment.[32] Maniotes highlights the continued importance of the search process model and the role of affective states in research with elementary students.[33] While it is acknowledged that K–2 students will likely not go through the entire inquiry process, they "can reflect on their learning by choosing an emoji or symbol that corresponds with their feelings through the process, especially in the early ages."[34] Even more significantly, emotions cue the learning team that a student needs additional support.[35]

As educators who see students across grade levels, librarians can enhance students' curiosity and reflectivity by ensuring the elementary curriculum in information literacy and inquiry moves students to increasing levels of autonomy. In *Inspiring Curiosity,* Cassinelli highlights the role of the librarian, from helping students confirm information to then leading them to structured, guided, and open or free inquiry.[36] Banchi and Bell noted that levels of inquiry are not determined by a child's age but rather by their experience with the inquiry process.[37] Examining information literacy through the inquiry process allows for the development of student understanding related to three key concepts: Information that is organized provides access to facts, ideas, and multiple perspectives; valuable information prompts curiosity, reflection, and enlightenment; and, thoughtfully interpreting information over time leads to deep learning.[38]

The American Association of School Librarians (AASL) Standards Framework for Learners, International Society for Technology in Education (ISTE) Standards, and the Future Ready Librarians Framework all highlight the importance of offering students opportunities to grow their social and emotional skills, which often comes through inquiry-based digital literacy and research-oriented tasks. The AASL learning standards emphasize the significance of students engaging in a research process that challenges them within an environment that fosters personal development.[39] Likewise, the ISTE Standards highlight the importance of the empowered learner who is motivated, self-directed, and constructively using feedback, fluent in digital tools, and socially and emotionally aware.[40] The Future Ready Librarians Framework notes that librarians provide "flexible spaces that promote inquiry, creativity, collaboration, and community."[41] Ultimately, students will benefit from being part of a school culture where risk-taking, trial and error, and potential failure can occur without shame or judgment. Librarians can help by fostering an environment that encourages creativity, resilience, and a growth mindset. The impact of using inquiry, research, and self-determined projects in information literacy cannot be overstated. Traditional research projects often do not offer transformational experiences with learning but instead focus on finding and reciting content.[42] The National Board Framework for Teachers highlights the importance of inquiry for creating transformative educational experiences for students: "Through inquiry, students search for problems, patterns, and solutions, making discoveries and advancing their own learning."[43]

INTEGRATING INFORMATION LITERACY INTO THE CURRICULUM

Information literacy instruction has primarily been led by finding ways to integrate the instruction within the traditional classroom curriculum or by implementing stand-alone lessons on information literacy topics. Other uses of information literacy instruction include the implementation of it within inquiry models or processes. Authentic curricula for information literacy are scarce but should consider aspects important to all types of pedagogy, such as universal design for learning, opportunities for practice, and appropriate scaffolding where needed. Finally, it is essential to consider ways in which the curricula connect with students' cognitive, social, and emotional growth, and their current needs in the digital world.

Students benefit from practice with digital tools and resources. They also learn most from high-quality digital content. Smith identifies key features of high-quality content as that in which children are engaged, outline purposeful learning goals, spark active experiences, and are socially involved. In addition, Smith notes that adults can facilitate these types of social, active engagements even if they are not immediately part of the digital experience. Furthermore, engaging students in active demonstrations of content they saw online helps them see the transferability of the content.[44]

Any instruction in information literacy benefits from other constructive pedagogical approaches, such as Vygotsky's Zone of Proximal Development (ZPD). ZPD, which focuses on meeting learners where they are, relates to scaffolding, which Kuhlthau notes is an essential part of a successful information search process.[45] In particular, scaffolding is more than just "help" in the information search process. In particular, Kuhlthau notes five levels of scaffolding that are appropriate at different times of interventions: organizer, lecturer, instructor, tutor, and counselor.

Scaffolding can be an education-based process, but it has also been seen in parent-child interactions and can be recreated with younger students in the classroom. Hammond, et al. found that parental scaffolding helped boost preschoolers' executive functioning. In particular, Joint Media Engagement (JME) involves co-viewing and interactive engagement of digital media between children and adults.[46] Utilizing JME helps scaffold and support children, and elevates the development of students' SEL skills and content knowledge.[47] Likewise, accomplished teachers scaffold inquiry for their students: "Accomplished educators model those processes for students, showing them how to pose problems and work through alternative solutions, as well as how to examine the answers that others have found to similar problems."[48]

Common Sense Media offers one of the few up-to-date K–12 curricula on Digital Citizenship based on the idea that "All students need digital citizenship skills to participate fully in their communities and make smart choices online and in life."[49] Their curriculum incorporates information literacy into its topic focus of news and media literacy, along with media balance, online privacy, digital footprint, communication, and cyberbullying. According to their research brief about the curriculum, the content was created not just to help students learn information and digital literacy at a level appropriate to their age and development, but to guide them through the challenges of living a modern-day digital life.[50]

In conclusion, librarians must be ready to support students in information literacy through scaffolded opportunities to discover, understand, and evaluate information. Understanding where a student comes from cognitively, socially, and emotionally is essential, as well as their background knowledge of digital tools and resources. Information literacy is key to lifelong learning, and the foundations can be set in the elementary years.

NOTES

1. American Library Association, "Presidential Committee on Information Literacy: Final Report," para. 3.
2. Katie Sherwin and Jacob Nielsen, "Children's UX: Usability Issues in Designing for Young People," para. 22.
3. Ibid, para 25.
4. Stépane Colognesi, "Listening Comprehension Is Not Innate to Elementary School Students," 10.
5. Iroise Dumontheil, "Development of Abstract Thinking during Childhood and Adolescence: The Role of Rostrolateral Prefrontal Cortex," 72.
6. Emilio Ferrer, Elizabeth O'Hare, and Silvia Bunge, "Fluid Reasoning and the Developing Brain," 48.
7. Allyson Mackey et al., "Differential Effects of Reasoning and Speed Training in Children."
8. Sherwin and Nielsen, "Children's UX: Usability Issues in Designing for Young People," 587.
9. Note: The ICDL, While Still in Existence Today, Does Not Utilize the Same Navigational Features It Had Prior to 2020, http://www.childrenslibrary.org.
10. Hilary Browne Hutchinson, Ben Bederson, and Allison Druin, "Children's Interface Design for Searching and Browsing," 110.
11. Stephanie Jones et al., "Executive Function Mapping Project: Untangling the Terms and Skills Related to Executive Function and Self-Regulation in Early Childhood," 1.
12. Anthony Anderson and Bill Johnston, *From Information Literacy to Social Epistemology: Insights from Psychology* (Kidlington: Chandos Publishing, 2016), 63.
13. Sherwin and Nielsen, "Children's UX: Usability Issues in Designing for Young People," Table 1.
14. Tatiana Gossen and Andreas Nürnberger, "Specifics of Information Retrieval for Young Users," 6.
15. Feifei Liu, "Designing for Kids: Cognitive Considerations," para 12.
16. Matt King, "Case Study 6: Navigating Databases with Digital Breadcrumbs."
17. Gossen and Nürnberger, "Specifics of Information Retrieval for Young Users," 6.
18. Liu, "Designing for Kids: Cognitive Considerations," para 12.
19. Committee for Children, "What Is Social-Emotional Learning?," para 1.
20. Libby Stanford and Caitlyn Meisner, "Social-Emotional Learning Persists Despite Political Backlash," para 10.
21. Lesley S. J. Farmer, "An Examination of the Correlation of Research Information Literacy Competence and Social-Emotional Behavior Among High School Students," 14.

22. Miriam Matteson and Omer Farooq, "Feeling Our Way: Emotional Intelligence and Information Literacy Competency," 204.

23. Julie Darling, *Social-Emotional Learning Using Makerspaces and Passion Projects* (New York, NY: Routledge, 2022).

24. Common Sense Education, *Everything You Need to Teach Digital Citizenship*, https://www.commonsense.org/education/digital-citizenship#:~:text=Everything%20You%20Need%20to%20Teach%20Digital%20Citizenship&text=Prepares%20students%20with%20critical%2021st,whole%20community%20through%20family%20outreach.

25. Carrie James, Emily Weinstein, and Kelly Mendoza, "Teaching Digital Citizens in Today's World: Research and Insights Behind the Common Sense K–12 Digital Citizenship Curriculum (Version 2)," 19.

26. The Nation's Report Card, https://www.nationsreportcard.gov/.

27. Gina Biancarosa and Gina Griffiths, "Technology Tools to Support Reading in the Digital Age," 143.

28. Sherwin and Nielsen, "Children's UX: Usability Issues in Designing for Young People," para 13.

29. James, Weinstein, and Mendoza, "Teaching Digital Citizens in Today's World: Research and Insights Behind the Common Sense K–12 Digital Citizenship Curriculum (Version 2)," 7.

30. Jennifer LaGarde and Darren Hudgins, *Fact vs. Fiction: Teaching Critical Thinking Skills in the Age of Fake News* (San Francisco, CA: International Society for Technology in Education, 2018), 64.

31. Tardiff, Anthony Bernard. "Have a CCOW: A CRAAP Alternative for the Internet Age." Journal of Information Literacy 16, no. 1 (June 1, 2022): 119–30. https://search.ebscohost.com/login.aspx?direct=true&db=eric&AN=EJ1347324&site=ehost-live.

32. Carol Kuhlthau, Leslie Maniotes, and Ann Caspari, *Guided Inquiry: Learning in the 21st Century* (Libraries Unlimited, 2015), 53–59.

33. Leslie Maniotes, *Guided Inquiry Design in Action: Elementary School* (United States: Libraries Unlimited, 2018), 5.

34. Ibid, 5.

35. Ibid, 5.

36. Colette Cassinelli, *Inspiring Curiosity: The Librarian's Guide to Inquiry-Based Learning* (United States: International Society for Technology in Education, 2018), 26–30.

37. Heather Banchi and Randy Bell, "The Many Levels of Inquiry," 29.

38. Kuhlthau, Maniotes, and Caspari, *Guided Inquiry: Learning in the 21st Century* (Santa Barbara, CA: Libraries Unlimited, 2015), 74–95.

39. American Association of School Librarians, *National School Library Standards for Learners, School Librarians, and School Libraries* (Chicago, IL: American Library Association, 2017).

40. Sarah Stoeckl, "Student Empowerment—From Vision to Practice."

41. All4Ed, "Future Ready Librarians Framework."

42. Kuhlthau, Maniotes, and Caspari, *Guided Inquiry: Learning in the 21st Century* (Santa Barbara, CA: Libraries Unlimited, 2015), 5.

43. National Board for Professional Teaching Standards, 21.

44. Smith, "Children, Executive Functioning, and Digital Media: A Review," 11.

45. Kuhlthau, "Students and the Information Search Process: Zones of Intervention for Librarians," 64–66.
46. Hammond et al., "The Effects of Parental Scaffolding on Preschoolers' Executive Function," 21–23.
47. H. Smith, "Children, Executive Functioning, and Digital Media: A Review," 9.
48. National Board for Professional Teaching Standards, 21.
49. Common Sense Education, *Everything You Need to Teach Digital Citizenship*, https://www.commonsense.org/education/digital-citizenship#:~:text=Everything%20You%20Need%20to%20Teach%20Digital%20Citizenship&text=Prepares%20students%20with%20critical%2021st,whole%20community%20through%20family%20outreach.
50. James, Weinstein, and Mendoza, "Teaching Digital Citizens in Today's World: Research and Insights Behind the Common Sense K–12 Digital Citizenship Curriculum (Version 2)," 48.

3

Preparing for the Unknown

MEDIA LITERACY IN ELEMENTARY SCHOOL

Katherine Counterman, Library Media Specialist, Katy, Texas

Little children have BIG emotions. Throughout elementary school, they start developing the vocabulary and neural connections needed to understand how these emotions affect and interact with their daily lives. There is a huge push for Social-Emotional Learning (SEL) in the younger grades around the country. Many definitions of SEL exist, but they all contain one basic principle—if students can understand and manage their emotions, they will be better suited to face challenges as an adult.[1] As all experienced elementary educators know, teaching students at this level involves modeling behavior as much as it involves imparting academic knowledge, if not more so.

THE ROLE OF MEDIA IN ELEMENTARY SCHOOL

From the shows they watch to the sites they visit to the billboards they see on the way to school, students' emotions are targeted through media messages on a daily basis. Even clothing can contain messages, carrying engaging slogans and/or logos to entice a purchase. Along with teaching how to evaluate information and cite their sources, elementary students need to understand what qualifies as media and how to evaluate it in its various forms. This is different from information literacy, which focuses on the evaluation of the information itself.

The 2020 Maryland School Librarian of the Year Donna Mignardi said it best: "The competencies our students need to make good decisions with the information they are exposed to need to be taught, modeled, and practiced continually."[2] In this post-pandemic educational climate, students are struggling with teacher turnover, increased social and emotional needs, and learning gaps.[3] Classroom teachers rarely have time to focus on media literacy, and most have little to no training on how to effectively teach it.

The school librarian, who sees all students on a weekly basis year after year, is in the perfect position to help guide children in this process. They can also provide professional development to classroom teachers and co-teach targeted media literacy lessons, developing a shared vocabulary that spans all grades in the school.

TEACHING MEDIA FORMATS IN THE ELEMENTARY LIBRARY

Before students can learn how to be media-literate, they must understand what falls under the umbrella of the term "media." The most impactful lesson regarding media that I do with my students every year is to pretend that I am psychic. I do this activity with all students in grades K–5 because I want it to be both an introduction to new students and a refresher for those who have seen this before. I start by choosing someone who is wearing expressive clothing. I ask them to stand up, and I "read their mind" by telling the class something the chosen student has never explicitly told me. For example, if the student is wearing a sparkly dress with a princess on it, I would say, "I know that you like princesses. I'm thinking that you probably also like unicorns?" This leads to discussions of how our choice of clothing can send messages as good as any form of the written word. I ask students to get into groups and practice being "psychic" by sharing something they know about each other based on an article of clothing. We then make lists of everything we can think of that sends a message, including street signs, brand icons, books, and television shows.

MEDIA LITERACY IN ELEMENTARY

The National Association for Media Literacy Education (NAMLE) defines media literacy as

> the ability to access, analyze, evaluate, create and act using all forms of communication. In its simplest terms, media literacy builds the foundation of upon traditional literacy and offers new forms of reading and writing. Media literacy empowers people to be critical thinkers and makers, effective communicators and active citizens.[4]

Considering the exponential rate at which opportunities for media creation develop, we need to prepare students to analyze and evaluate sources that do not yet exist. Until the late twentieth century, the general public had very few

Katherine Counterman

methods available for gathering information. In 1993, the first publicly accessible web browser—Mosaic—was developed.[5] Thirty years later, we live in an Information Age in which people carry a computer in their pocket with instantaneous access to the internet. We can only guess what will be available when current kindergarten students reach adulthood.

Having a librarian leading the way in media literacy instruction opens the door for a cohesive, effective learning environment for students of all ages.

TEACHING MEDIA LITERACY IN THE ELEMENTARY LIBRARY

The biggest concept to teach the youngest learners is that not everything they read or see is a fact. I work with my kindergarten and first-grade students on this idea. I pair the book *A Goofy Guide to Penguins* by Jean-Luc Coudray and Phillippe Coudray with a nonfiction penguin book (any easy reader will do). First, I read a nonfiction book about penguins. As a class, we record facts that we learned. Then, I read *A Goofy Guide to Penguins*. We check it against the facts learned from the previous book. The book gets progressively sillier, and students usually catch on that something is wrong near the middle. Finally, we compare everything we've read with an article about penguins from a research database (I like to use PebbleGo by Capstone, but you could use any online encyclopedia). This leads to discussions on the author's purpose.

As students get older, I focus on how to evaluate sources through the lens of research. Likening the research process to completing a puzzle, I prominently display the words "source," "credible," and "cite" in the initial presentation. These words are then added to the library word wall for reference.

Most students do not need direct instruction in questioning the reliability of media sources. I typically rely on students to catch the discrepancies when I use false information websites, such as www.allaboutexplorers.com and zapatopi.net/treeoctopus/. My job there is to scaffold the nine-, ten-, and eleven-year-olds into noticing the inconsistencies on their own. What isn't inherent, however, is the knowledge that facts can change. A book written in 1995 about the solar system wasn't incorrect when it defined Pluto as a planet. A map produced in the late 1970s identifying the Union of Soviet Socialist Republics wasn't created to trick anyone. Young children do not instinctively know this and must be explicitly taught.

My library classroom has six tables. To teach the concepts of information fluidity and how copyright dates affect information reliability, I place one of the following on each table:

- a globe produced in the 1960s
- an autobiography of Princess Diana, copyright 1984

- a postcard featuring the New York City skyline with the Twin Towers prominently displayed
- a technology reference book, copyright 1991
- a laptop displaying a current article on Tyrannosaurus Rex from Encyclopaedia Britannica
- a laptop displaying a current article on Tyrannosaurus Rex from PebbleGo

Students are assigned their first table, I set a timer for two minutes, and their set of instructions includes only one task: observe the media and record one thing that interests you. At the end of two minutes, the groups switch to the next table and perform the same task. This continues until twelve minutes pass and students have rotated to each table.

For the second part of the lesson, I project five images and go through them one at a time. Students view a current world map, a current view of the NYC skyline, a screenshot of a current news article featuring Prince Philip, a side-by-side comparison of T-Rex illustrations from the Britannica and PebbleGo articles, and a timeline of the evolution of the telephone that spans its creation until today. Every year, students are blown away by the idea that everything they just viewed either is currently fact or was considered fact at the time of publication. Especially interesting to them is that despite one of the T-Rex illustrations depicting the dinosaur as having feathers while the other does not, they are both currently considered correct based on the evolving information gleaned by scientists. Since my goal is to ignite the concept in their growing minds, we do not delve much deeper than the idea that factual information presented by any media type can change. However, I continue to stoke the flames by weaving it in throughout the year.

INCORPORATING MEDIA LITERACY IN THE ELEMENTARY LIBRARY YEAR-ROUND

With the potential to work with students for six years as they transition from kindergarten to fifth grade, school librarians have the unique ability to ensure the continuity of teaching media literacy. In a school with an enrollment of approximately 900 students, I teach all children for thirty minutes every other week. However, I make sure all classes come to the library to exchange books every week, along with providing passes to teachers for open checkout every day. Every time a student sets foot in the library, it is a chance to embed media literacy. The following are more ideas to incorporate the subject year-round:

- If a student wants to share a "fact" they learned, ask them the source of that fact, and question them on the source's reliability.

- When reading a book to students, take a moment to review the copyright page and think about whether the publication year matters when considering the text.
- Have a corner of the library dedicated to a "fact of the week," citing the source and displaying it, if possible. Rotate between various forms of media, such as websites, books, maps, etc.
- Intentionally wear clothing that students can "read" and spark conversation. My favorite way to do this is with earrings featuring popular characters.
- Put daily calendars of varying topics at the circulation desk (I have five). As students wait to check out, they can learn facts, view art, discover jokes, and much more! Once the day has passed, I use the pages as incentives. The best time to pick up calendars is at the end of January/beginning of February when they are at a deep discount.

INTENTIONALITY AND CONSISTENCY ARE KEY IN ELEMENTARY SCHOOL

Creating a school library program immersed in media literacy does not happen overnight. It has taken me eleven years to get to where I am now, and I don't think I will ever stop adding to and tweaking lessons in my repertoire. The key to succeeding in teaching media literacy to elementary students is to be intentional and consistent with exposure to various media forms. The only way for young children to move toward evaluating and creating media themselves is for them to recognize it without our guidance, and since media is continuously evolving, we have a responsibility to our students to evolve with it.

NOTES

1. Berg, Juliette, et al. "The Intersection of School Climate and Social and Emotional Development." American Institutes for Research, February 2017, https://www.air.org/sites/default/files/2021-06/Intersection-School-Climate-and-Social-and-Emotional-Development-February-2017.pdf.
2. Mignardi, Donna. "Graduating Information- and Media-Literate Students." *Knowledge Quest* 50, no. 2 (2021): 9–14.
3. Gabryel, Carleigh. "The Impact of Increased Teacher Turnover." University of North Carolina Research, December 13, 2022, https://research.unc.edu/2022/12/13/the-impact-of-increased-teacher-turnover/.
4. "Media Literacy Defined." National Association for Media Literacy Education, November 15, 2023, https://namle.net/resources/media-literacy-defined/.
5. Goldsborough, Reid. "A Quarter Century of the Graphical Web." *Teacher Librarian* 45, no. 4 (2018): 62.

4

Health Literacy for Young Children

Eleanor Layo Freed, Material and Self-Fashioning
Literacy Specialist, Berkeley, California

The vast majority of chronic diseases (about 80 percent) are preventable "if we start in infancy and raise our children on the principles of Lifestyle Medicine."[1] Libraries play a crucial role in helping children learn how to be healthy. Early health literacy improves students' quality of life for their whole lives. Younger children may use "Critical Health Literacy" (CHL). CHL requires children to plan and evaluate their interpersonal actions toward health.[2] Post-COVID-19 research shows that young children already self-identify as health agents for their families, their community, and themselves—even without functional literacy skills.[3] School libraries train CHL with activities that directly engage children's bodies and social capacities with fun and imagination-rich experiences.

LIFESTYLE MEDICINE

This chapter helps you train CHL in children ages three to ten using models developed within Lifestyle Medicine (LM).[4] LM is an evolving practice of doctors certified by The American College of Lifestyle Medicine (ACLM) that covers all ages of children and adults. Health insurance agencies, health educators, and organizations worldwide are depending increasingly on LM for metadata, communications, and best practices, and those professionals expect libraries to be active partners.

The LM framework[5] has seven pillars: movement and fitness, healthful nutrition, restorative sleep, stress management, social engagement, gratitude reflection, and cognitive enhancement.[6] These pillars support elements such as bone density, brain nerve networks, muscles, social senses, spiritual-emotional capacities, and more. The process of health literacy involves simple practices and strongly correlates with habit formation.[7] These habits build children's skills and enable their social engagements to be effective, immediate, and healthy. The activities and practices in this chapter are organized by the LM seven-pillar framework.[8]

Poor childhood development in these areas often results in preventable chronic diseases, as shown by alarming increases in occurrence at younger ages each decade since 1988.[9] Health literacy is urgent, valuable, and easy to conduct in libraries using the LM framework. The following list describes activities for health literacy following the seven LM pillars:

- One—Movement and fitness: Fairy house building
- Two—Healthful nutrition: Fruit touch and taste
- Three—Restorative Sleep: Stuffed animal sleepover
- Four—Stress Management: Fashion coping
- Five—Social Engagement: Sound stories
- Six—Gratitude and Reflection: Tree of kindness
- Seven—Cognitive Enhancement: Musical chairs roleplay

ONE—MOVEMENT FITNESS

Activity: Fairy House Building

Host a walk-through of child-made fairy houses and park them inside the nooks of the library for discovery games.

Fairy houses are little settings put along sidewalk foliage, parks, and open spaces. To build them, suggest local, abundant items that are simple, affordable, and reusable, or free supplies such as popsicle sticks and matchboxes. Gather select natural items such as dry lichen for house details on stairs, doors, and windows. In urban settings, consider a fairy house search walk. Social interaction during outdoor time where features such as trees and fungi abound may visually spark imaginative ideas, for instance, on the life of fairies living in trees and under mushrooms.

Los Angeles resident Rita Tateel began building a fairy world on a sidewalk tree, and it became a source of joy and a place for children to participate and contribute.[10] East Wenatchee, Washington, resident Bonnie Grant, as another example, used her deep knowledge of children from her thirty-one years of managing a school counseling office to expand her fairy house wall to help kids cope with the various stresses of COVID-19.[11]

BEST PRACTICES FOR PILLAR #1: MOVEMENT AND FITNESS

Children generate faith and hope by using fairy stories, according to researcher and child psychologist Steven Walker.[12] These are excellent long-term strategies for health literacy.

Fairy house-making protects children against negative influences such as those from products marketed to them—and in frequent use by them—designed with specific intent to seduce, addict, and preoccupy. Current lawsuits are challenging these negative consequences,[13] yet we cannot wait for the lengthy process of legal protections to become policy and then be implemented by families before we take preventive action like introducing children to fairy house creation. The history of health-harming products confirms this need.[14]

To immediately counter these unfair pulls on children's desires, help them form habits of choosing movement activities such as seeking fairy houses around neighborhoods and libraries. Fairy houses have become popular in many cities globally and are a welcome addition to any neighborhood, making this a sustainable pastime that boosts health throughout childhood and adolescence.

TWO—HEALTHFUL NUTRITION

Activity: Fruit Touch and Taste

Host a tactile fruit party comparing hand feel and mouthfeel.

The activity begins with a hands-on exploration of whole, uncut fruits hidden in paper bags. Without looking, children feel in the bags to guess what fruits are inside. If they can't name them, they may invent a name, draw a picture, or view pictures of fruits to find a match. Include unusual and available seasonal fruits.

Next, children make their own fruit salad by selecting from cut fruits laid out in separate bowls arranged by color. Color is the key to nutritional benefit. "The most vibrantly colored fruits and vegetables are the richest in vitamins, minerals, fiber and antioxidants," according to RUSH University Medical Center.[15] Children learn the value of variety as they pay attention to the mouthfeel of each fruit.

To deepen their understanding, ask children to compare their experience using hands and mouth. If time allows, add tasting combinations such as cheese, as recommended by Berkeley, California's Cheese Board Collective co-owner Eric, who explains how added fat pairs well with the acidity of fruits.

Best Practices for Pillar #2: Healthful Nutrition

The most important factor in nutrition health literacy for young children is positive associations with eating diverse fruits and vegetables.[16] Active child participation in preparing the foods they eat is an excellent habit to instill early.

Now the children are health ambassadors. Their newly gained ability to discuss this universal, simple, yet sophisticated topic builds in them a diverse interaction potential that can bridge generations, socioeconomics, cultures, geographies, and invisible health differences such as allergies or digestive disorders like Crohn's disease.

For playful versions of this exercise, have children describe the fruits most enjoyed by imaginary folk such as fairies, aliens, or video and storybook characters. Hand-feel vs. mouthfeel is a lifelong exploration, making it a stabilizing habit of mind to start early.

THREE—RESTORATIVE SLEEP

Activity: Stuffed Animal Sleepover

Host a sleepover inside the library with a tent or shelter and a music player or cell phone.

A week or two prior to the sleepover, share with participants a variety of music and ambient sounds proven to be helpful for restorative sleep, such as the nature sounds of rain or acoustic music.[17] To locate free internet materials, try the search prompt, "restorative music for children's sleep free,"[18] or source from freesound.org. Present participants with at least three music choices. Nature sounds are good as one of those choices. For the sleepover, ask children to pretend they are an adult offering soothing and positive expectations of a restorative night's sleep to their stuffed animal with them explaining that a special sound mix will help sleep be good and healthy.

Compile a playlist from the children's preferred selections. Archiving the playlist for the benefit of year-on-year programming builds a unique life history for children connected to their childhood library, a place that "they remember and that remembers them." Playlists may also be explored by children to try at home as they reach for enhanced sleep.

Next, children are ready to do the sleepover themselves. Hosting one for first-t to fifth-graders is made easy by the checklists provided by librarian Linda Stover of Everett, Washington, available on the internet and free.[19]

Best Practices for Pillar #3: Restorative Sleep

Poor sleep derives from and contributes to myriad problems during childhood, such as anxiety, poor concentration, and lack of consistent sleep hygiene.[20] For example, one healthy habit is to unplug from all electronic screen stimulation at least a half hour before bedtime rituals start (such as teeth-brushing, pajamas, hug-talks, and bedtime stories). While light and visual stimulation are problematic,[21] the opposite is true for audio.[22] Soundscapes can aid sleep and solidify bedtime ritual consistency.

Music is relatable for children of every age. Evidence continues to mount that select music and sounds are effective self-soothing wake-to-sleep transition tools throughout life.[23,24] Music during naps may even help.[25] While research suggests specific sounds proven in studies, personal resonance and the feelings of each individual are the ultimate judge, meaning a child's preferences are important to test and confirm through guided experimentation.

FOUR—STRESS MANAGEMENT

Activity: Fashion Coping

Host a bling party where children discover the non-verbal messaging power of accessorizing.

Place containers in the middle of a table with affordable items like costume jewelry, charity shop hats, scarves, and eyewear. Ask each child to select an item and accessorize with something that they would normally never wear. Next, they sit around the table, and the group looks at one child at a time, saying how the object changes their look or evokes a way they might act. This exercise is most interesting when the children go way out of character with the object they select and when the children already know each other well, so that they have the experience of not recognizing their friend now that they have worn the new item as a fashion accessory.

Best Practices for Pillar #4: Stress Management

Fashion coping, a phrase coined by me, is an everyday destressing mechanism extensively used by adolescents. Young children have the freedom to experiment, and this exercise helps them be ready to express themselves intentionally by their teen years. Children with a self-fashioning sense are alert to using attire accessories to spot others with similar affinities to themselves. The library health literacy program is a good place for this method of destressing by fashioning oneself with a single accessory because the library is a *third place* with low bias and low peer pressure.

Children learn that fashion can be self-controlled, affordably achieved, and used to cope and feel empowered. As a health habit, children learn they are their own agents of change and may use the act of self-fashioning to satisfy the need to confirm that they matter, and that they are their own agents in communicating how they matter.[26] Providing a socially neutral fashioning milieu, the library trains children in new ways to process feelings and experiment with identity.

FIVE—SOCIAL ENGAGEMENT

Activity: Sound Stories

Children author stories and speak them into recording devices for the library to share on-site.

Use audio recording devices such as cell phones to capture stories told by youth. These may be first drafts or more developed works. Next, set up a desk as a mock publishing house. Host author events and play excerpts. Invite other authors, library staff, and teen volunteers. Once the children have completed one full loop of creation-publishing-reflection-re-creation, their sense of audience experience will surface. See if children exclaim as they watch audiences hear their work: "I never thought someone would take it like that!"

A health-habit opportunity from this activity is critical thinking to inform questions such as: How do we decide when to incorporate community and peer feedback? When do we stick to personal wants and what feels right for the author's voice to ring true? When is resistance to the group opinion futile, and when is resistance fertile? In addressing these questions as a group, the potential for friendships emerges, and friendships are known to be important to children's well-being.[27]

Best Practices for Pillar #5: Social Engagement

Full-loop oration (FLO), a phrase coined by me, describes the aforementioned fast-tracking of community feedback as an author develops a story. FLO is designed to minimize emotional risk by starting sharing while the invested effort is small. Social engagement as a full loop—draft, share, listen, rewrite, add visuals, share, listen, add sounds, share, listen, and so on—supports health in for young children by making them an integral part of their community, adding to a feeling that they matter and likewise making their community a part of their storytelling.

Even very young children can compose and share their stories even before they can read and write.[28] Functional literacy is not a prerequisite to authoring, nor for CHL.[29] CHL skills help children make engaging stories, too, as storytelling involves a plan and evaluation of interpersonal actions.

This health pillar of social engagement of developing self-authored stories enables children to find and keep friends as an authoring social group that creates child culture and sustains positive social ties at their library. Research shows that success builds anticipation of success; this makes early library group social dynamics crucial to children's later eagerness to work in groups.[30]

SIX—GRATITUDE AND REFLECTION

Activity: Tree of Kindness

Install a tree structure and invite children to attach "leaves" that list their acts of kindness.

Initially, children must be guided to do a random act of kindness, such as complimenting a cafeteria worker or picking up a paper that fell from someone's backpack.[31] The tree symbolizes a connection between kindness and gratitude. After the tree is well-populated with notes, stage a "leaf falling" performance emphasizing the acts themselves while underplaying who did them. The health habit to build is *giving is an act of receiving.*

Best Practices for Pillar #6: Gratitude and Reflection

Using the metaphor of a tree naturalizes positive social behaviors. This is more concrete than many acts of gratitude we ask children to perform, such as saying *thank you.* Genuine feelings of appreciation happen alongside feelings of satisfaction. However, satisfaction does not come naturally. The opposite is true. As Australian sociologist Hugh Mackay reports from many years of research, people have an innate yearning for more, more, more![32] The tree of kindness offers satisfaction of a job well done, of belonging and of being relevant. In turn, those satisfactions support gratitude and reflection.

One health skill built during the tree of kindness activity is what I call *conspicuously celebrating*—a play on the concept of conspicuous consumption (CC).[33] CC is where secondary signals to anonymous others build a cultural climate associated with a particular place. The library, in this case, is the place associated with kindness and appreciation as host of the tree and venue of the performance.

Resources to supplement this activity include: (1) stories on post-COVID-19 perspectives on friendships among children;[34] (2) Academy Award-winning best short film 2023 and companion book, *The Boy, the Mole, the Fox and the Horse;*[35] and, (3) the Discord channel on random acts of kindness.[36]

SEVEN—COGNITIVE ENHANCEMENT

Activity: Musical Chairs Roleplay

Play musical chairs with a twist. Each chair turns a child into the role marked on the seat.

Children try on various social perspectives as they become the dad, the big sister, the teacher, or the town mayor. Is candy healthy if it reduces your stress? Is being there for a new game that starts at 4 a.m. healthier than meeting sleep needs because it builds friendships? Some would argue *yes,* others *no.*

Run musical chairs by the normal rules. The "out" child who has not captured a chair becomes the game master who chooses which two seated children must debate the topic announced by the librarian for thirty seconds. Explain to the children that they should argue not how they really feel but pretend they are a person with the role marked on their seat.

Best Practices for Pillar #7: Cognitive Enhancement

Cognitive reappraisal (CR) is a strategic technique used in therapy and beyond for emotional self-regulation.[37] CR skills are useful at all ages, including ages 3–10 for coping, recovery, and point-of-view flexibility. CR helps children cope with mental and cognitive challenges.[38] Cognitive reappraisal skills are learned as children debate health issues from different points of view during roleplay. CR skills grow during social perspective-taking. Roleplay pretending is a type of fiction that works for social-emotional learning, which children must develop out of school contexts such as libraries, as validated in the field of Pediatric Occupational Therapy.[39] This enables viewpoint-shifting, a cognitive tool the children will then have available for their lifelong critical thinking and editing work. It will help in academic work, relationships, conflict resolution, trauma recovery, and adaptability in times of change.

With this musical chairs roleplay, children will develop CR skills by seeing situations from fresh perspectives. Trauma reduction is an example where this is helpful. Children who learn CR early can later utilize it reflexively for tough mental tasks, such as overcoming a stressful memory.[40] They learn to look at previous situations in a new way. In turn, this grows new brain pathways to better associations that will make the same old memory have more pleasure during the next recall.[41] The effects benefit a child's memorization ability. In one study to validate CR, a group of children were shown a movie, and the ones with skills in CR had better recall.[42]

Forgetting is not the reverse of remembering. Disappearing a prior experience is not an option. Relief, however, is possible, and CR is a proven effective tool for a problematic memory,[43] and helps children in school with ADHD by early adolescence.[44]

CONCLUSION

Libraries can readily create health literacy curriculum using LM, because it requires what librarians do best, such as filtering fake information, finding up-to-date information, providing self-direction support, facilitating healthy choice-making, competency training, and keeping it fun. According to research, schools are the best place for health literacy.[45] These facts combined suggest your school library is the top spot to spearhead this training. The activities in this chapter allow you to start training using the trending and highly regarded LM seven-pillar framework with which you are now familiar.

Your community will want validating facts, so here are a few examples:

- In the United States, children are currently deriving nearly 70 percent of their calories from ultra-processed foods;[46]
- One in three children in the United States are overweight or obese, cor-related to Type 2 diabetes increases;[47]
- Threats like inadequate diets are causing lower IQs and deficits in brain architecture;
- Health literacy has resulted in significant positive outcomes, as seen in recent lower smoking rates;[48]

- Children under three need to eat plenty of fat-rich nuts and seeds, in addition to fruits and vegetables;[49]
- U.S. annual health care spending grew 4.1 percent in 2022, reaching $4.5 trillion or $13,493 per person, up from $4.1 trillion in 2017 when 90 percent of those costs were for chronic and mental health condition expenditures.[50] This is why doctors now hand out "social prescriptions."[51]

Health literacy work is funded because these negatives are preventable.[52,53] Evidence is also available to substantiate your needs for staff training in health literacy.[54]

Teachers, parents, and health professionals all rely on librarians for updating and verifying information, designing activities, and locating step-by-step methods to imbue health intelligence into young children. Collateral for promotions is freely available from the ACLM.[55] New training items are regularly published on the internet because mental, spiritual, and physical health are now trending hot topics. LM curricula for adolescents, such as the "Lifestyle Medicine for Teens" micro-credential, is available for free.[56] Teens completing the credential will need volunteer hours that your program may provide while teens also gain free help.

Health literacy provided by librarians saves lives, saves money, and increases life joy.

NOTES

1. Dexter Shurney and Paula Gustafson, "Lifestyle Medicine in Children," *American Journal of Lifestyle Medicine*, 14, no. 1 (November 3, 2019): 54. DOI: 10.1177/1559827619879090.
2. Catherine Jenkins, Susie Sykes, and Jane Wills, "Public Libraries as Supportive Environments for Children's Development of Critical Health Literacy," *International Journal of Environmental Research and Public Health*, 19, no. 19 (September 20, 2022): 1–14. DOI: 10.3390/ijerph19191189.
3. Jenkins, Sykes, and Wills, "Public Libraries as Supportive Environments for Children's Development of Critical Health Literacy," 1.
4. Melissa Sundermann, Deborah Chielli, and Susan Spell, "Nature as Medicine: The 7th (Unofficial) Pillar of Lifestyle Medicine," *American Journal of Lifestyle Medicine*, 17, no. 5 (2023): 717–729. DOI: 10.1177/15598276231174863.
5. Michelle Dalal, Yamileth Cazorla-Lancaster, Cherie Chu, and Neeta Agarwal, "Healthy From the Start-Lifestyle Interventions in Early Childhood," *American Journal of Lifestyle Medicine*, 16, no. 5 (May 24, 2022): 562–569. DOI: 10.1177/15598276221087672.
6. "Lifestyle Medicine Pillars," Stanford Center on Longevity, Stanford University, January 23, 2024, https://longevity.stanford.edu/lifestyle/lifestyle-pillars/.
7. Charles Duhigg, *The Power of Habit: What We Do What We Do In Life and Business* (New York: Random House, 2012), 63, 283.

8. Dalal et al., "Healthy From the Start-Lifestyle Interventions in Early Childhood," 562–569.

9. Gabrielle Miller, Edward Coffield, Zanie Leroy, and Robin Wallin, "Prevalence and Costs of Five Chronic Conditions in Children," *The Journal of School Nursing*, 32, no. 5 (October 2016): 358. DOI: 10.1177/1059840516641190.

10. Jeanette Masrantos, "A Whimsical, Magical Fairy Tree Brings Smiles to an L.A. Neighborhood," *Los Angeles Times*, October 6, 2017, https://www.latimes.com/home/garden/la-hm-magical-fairy-tree-20171007-story.html.

11. Don Seabrook, "Fairy Garden Helps Deal with Coronavirus," *The Wenatchee (Wash.) World*, August 14, 2020, https://shorturl.at/dwx16.

12. Steven Walker, "Young People's Mental Health: The Spiritual Power of Fairy Stories, Myths and Legends," *Mental Health, Religion & Culture*, 13 (2010): 81–92.

13. Angus Crawford and Tony Smith, "I Was Addicted to Social Media - Now I'm Suing Big Tech," *BBC News*, November 19, 2023, https://www.bbc.com/news/technology-67443705.

14. Joel Bakan, *Childhood Under Siege: How Big Business Targets Your Children* (New York: Simon and Schuster, 2011), 11.

15. "Eat a Colorful Diet," RUSH University Medical Center, Accessed February 17, 2024, https://shorturl.at/gkCK3.

16. Isabella Skye Waddell and Caroline Orfila, "Dietary Fiber in the Prevention of Obesity and Obesity-Related Chronic Diseases: From Epidemiological Evidence to Potential Molecular Mechanisms," *Critical Reviews in Food Science and Nutrition*, 63, 8752–8767. DOI: 10.1080/10408398.2022.2061909.

17. Sandee LaMotte, "White Noise (and Pink and Brown): The Science Behind the Sounds," *CNN*, March 18, 2021, https://www.cnn.com/2021/03/18/health/white-pink-brown-noise-sleep-wellness/index.html.

18. "Restorative Music for Children Sleep Free," Google, https://www.google.com/search?q=restorative+music+for+children+sleep+free&oq=restorative+music+for+children+sleep+free.

19. Linda Stover, "Hosting a Library Sleepover," Evergreen Branch Library, Everett Public Library, Washington Library Association, 1–18, https://www.wla.org/assets/WALE/2014Conference/SessionHandouts/hosting%20a%20library%20sleepover.pdf.

20. Les Gellis and Kenneth Lichstein, "Sleep Hygiene Practices of Good and Poor Sleepers in the United States: An Internet-Based Study," *Behavior Therapy*, 40, no. 1 (March 2009): 1–9. DOI: 10.1016/j.beth.2008.02.001.

21. Emily Ricketts, Daniel Joyce, Ariel Rissman, Helen Burgess, Christopher Colwell, Leon Lack, and Michael Gradisar, "Electric Lighting, Adolescent Sleep and Circadian Outcomes, and Recommendations for Improving Light Health," *Sleep Medicine Reviews*, 64 (August 12, 2022): 1–4. DOI: 10.1016/j.smrv.2022.101667.

22. Maren Cordi, Sandra Ackermann, and Björn Rasch, "Effects of Relaxing Music on Healthy Sleep," *Scientific Reports* 9, no. 9079 (June 24, 2019): 1–10. DOI: 10.1038/s41598-019-45608-y.

23. Lyz Cooper, "Music to Make Sleep Problems a Thing of the Past," *British Academy of Sound Therapy*, April 25, 2017, https://britishacademyofsoundtherapy.com/sleep-problems/.

24. "Public Missing Out on a Night's Worth of Sleep Every Week," Royal Society for Public Health (RSPH), Accessed January 30, 2024, https://www.rsph.org.uk/our -work/policy/wellbeing/sleep.html.

25. Cordi, Ackermann, and Rasch, "Effects of Relaxing Music on Healthy Sleep," 1–10.

26. Hugh Mackay, *What Makes Us Tick: Making Sense of Who We Are and the Desires That Drive Us* (Sydney: Hachette Australia, 2019), 2–35.

27. Amanda Rose, Sarah Borowski, Allie Spiekerman, and Rhiannon Smith, "Children's Friendships," in *The Wiley-Blackwell Handbook of Childhood Social Development*, 3rd ed. (Wiley-Blackwell, 2022). DOI: 10.1002/9781119679028.ch26.

28. Barbara Ann Henderson, "Voice Lessons — On Becoming an Author: A Developmental Study of Fiction Writing in a First-Second Grade Urban Classroom" (PhD Dissertation, Stanford University, Stanford, CA, 1996).

29. Jenkins, Sykes, and Wills, "Public Libraries as Supportive Environments for Children's Development of Critical Health Literacy," 1.

30. Carolyn Anderson and Scott Myers, *The Fundamentals of Small Group Communication*, 1st ed. (Los Angeles, CA: SAGE Publications, Inc., 2008), 127–140.

31. Jennifer Taylor, "100 Random Acts of Kindness Ideas," *SignUpGenius,* February 15, 2023, https://www.signupgenius.com/groups/random-acts-of-kindness -ideas.cfm.

32. Mackay, *What Makes Us Tick: Making Sense of Who We Are and the Desires that Drive Us*, 2–35.

33. Georgios Patsiaouras and James Fitchett, "The Evolution of Conspicuous Consumption," *Journal of Historical Research in Marketing*, 4, no. 1 (January 27, 2012): 154–176. DOI: 10.1108/17557501211195109.

34. Danaë Larivière-Bastien, Oliver Aubuchon, Aubuchon Blondin, Dominique Dupont, Jamie Libenstein, Florence Séguin, Alexandra Tremblay, Hamza Zarglayoun, Catherine Herba, and Miriam Beauchamp, "Childrens Perspectives on Friendships and Socialization During the COVID-19 Pandemic: A Qualitative Approach," *Child Care Health Development*, 48, no. 6 (November 2022): 1017–1030. DOI: 10.1111/ cch.12998.

35. Charlie Mackesy, *The Boy, the Mole, the Fox and the Horse* (New York: HarperOne, 2019).

36. "Random Acts of Kindness on Discord (RAOKs)," Raokd, Mattel Creations, January 22, 2023, https://community.creations.mattel.com/forums/topic/133464-raokd -from-discord/?ct=1676450750.

37. David Clark, "Cognitive Reappraisal," *Cognitive and Behavioral Practice*, 29, no. 3 (August 2022): 564–566. DOI: 10.1016/j.cbpra.2022.02.018.

38. Madhuleena Roy Chowdhury, "Emotional Regulation: 6 Key Skills to Regulate Emotions," *PositivePsychology*, August 11, 2023, https://positivepsychology.com/emotion-regulation/.

39. Cristin Tilki, "Storying: An OT-Informed Framework for the Development of Cognitive Reappraisal in School-Age Children" (PhD Dissertation, Boston University, ProQuest), 24, https://shorturl.at/cklz3.

40. Cynthia Willner, Jessica Hoffmann, Craig Bailey, Alexandra Harrison, Beatris Garcia, Zi Jia Ng, Christina Cipriano, and Marc Brackett, "The Development of Cognitive Reappraisal From Early Childhood Through Adolescence: A Systematic Review

and Methodological Recommendations," *Frontiers in Psychology*, 13 (June 22, 2022). DOI: 10.3389/fpsyg.2022.875964.

41. Chowdhury, "Emotional Regulation: 6 Keys to Regulate Emotions."
42. Elizabeth Davis and Linda Levine, "Emotion Regulation Strategies That Promote Learning: Reappraisal Enhances Children's Memory for Educational Information," *Child Development*, 84, no. 1 (January-February 2013): 361–374. DOI: 10.1111/j.1467-8624.2012.01836.x.
43. Chowdhury, "Emotional Regulation: 6 Keys to Regulate Emotions."
44. Xiaoyu Lan, Chunhua Ma, and Yongfeng Ma, "'Three Pills' (Cognitive Reappraisal × Social Support × Cognitive Flexibility) and Their Impact on ADHD Symptoms in Early Adolescence: Synergistic or Compensatory Effect?," *Personality and Individual Differences*, 211 (September 2023). DOI: 10.1016/j.paid.2023.112246.
45. Manuela Pulimeno, Prisco Piscitelli, Salvatore Colazzo, Annamaria Colao, and Alessandro Miani, "School as Ideal Setting to Promote Health and Wellbeing Among Young People," *Health Promotion Perspectives*, 10, no. 4 (November 7, 2020): 316–324. DOI: 10.34172/hpp.2020.50.
46. Lu Wang, Euridice Martínez Steele, Mengxi Du, Jennifer Pomeranz, Lauren O'Connor, Kirsten Herrick, Hanqi Luo, Xuehong Zhang, Dariush Mozaffarian, and Fang Fang Zhang, "Trends in Consumption of Ultraprocessed Foods Among U.S. Youths Aged 2-19 Years, 1999-2018," *JAMA*, 326, no. 6 (August 10, 2021): 519–530. DOI: 10.1001/jama.2021.10238.
47. Marjorie McCullough, Diane Feskanich, Meir Stampfer, Edward Giovannucci, Eric Rimm, Frank Hu, Donna Spiegelman, David Hunter, Graham Colditz, and Walter Willett, "Diet Quality and Major Chronic Disease Risk in Men and Women: Moving Toward Improved Dietary Guidance," *The American Journal of Clinical Nutrition*, 76, no. 6 (December 2002): 1261–1271. DOI: 10.1093/ajcn/76.6.1261.
48. Shurney and Gustafson, "Lifestyle Medicine in Children," 54–56.
49. Dalal et al., "Healthy From the Start-Lifestyle Interventions in Early Childhood," 562–569.
50. Centers for Medicare & Medicaid Services, "National Health Expenditure Data: Historical," December 13, 2023, https://www.cms.gov/Research-Statistics-Data -and-Systems/Statistics-Trends-and-Reports/NationalHealthExpendData/Nat ionalHealthAccountsHistorical.
51. Katrina Hough, Ashwin Kotwal, Cynthia Boyd, Soe Han Tha, and Carla Perissinotto, "What Are 'Social Prescriptions' and How Should They Be Integrated Into Care Plans?" *AMA Journal of Ethics*, 25, no. 11 (November 2023): E795–E801.
52. Christine Buttorff, Teague Ruder, and Melissa Bauman, "Multiple Chronic Conditions in the United States" (Santa Monica, CA: RAND Corporation, 2017), https:// www.rand.org/content/dam/rand/pubs/tools/TL200/TL221/RAND_TL221.pdf.
53. Centers for Medicare & Medicaid Services, "National Health Expenditure Data."
54. Evgenia Vassilakaki and Valentini Moniarou-Papaconstaninou, "Librarians' Support in Improving Health Literacy: A Systematic Literature Review," *Journal of Librarianship and Information Science*, 55, no. 2 (May 5, 2022): 500–514. DOI: 10.1177/09610006221093794.

55. "Resources & Recommendations," American College of Lifestyle Medicine (ACLM), Accessed January 30, 2024, https://connect.lifestylemedicine.org/lmigtoolkit/new-page513/new-page4.

56. Kathryn Lytton, "HSC Launches First-of-its-Kind Lifestyle Medicine for Teens Microcredential," The University of North Texas Health Science Center at Fort Worth, August 3, 2023, https://www.unthsc.edu/newsroom/story/hsc-launches-first-of-its-kind-lifestyle-medicine-for-teens-microcredential/.

5

Information Literacy in Middle School

BORN TO RESEARCH

Beth Thomas, School Library Media Specialist,
Lawton C. Johnson Summit Middle School, New Jersey

Today's sixth to eighth graders (and even some of their parents) have been surrounded by technology since the day they were born. From that day on, they have become accustomed to having memories and milestones recorded with cell phone cameras and have likely effortlessly scrolled and swiped a tablet or phone starting when they were toddlers. In his 2001 paper, "Digital Natives, Digital Immigrants," Marc Prensky introduced the concept of the "digital native," people born after 1980 who have grown up immersed in technology.[1] The label "digital native" took on a life of its own, with many people equating digital nativism with being an expert evaluator of information encountered online. However, just because a person has been immersed in technology doesn't mean that they can easily navigate all aspects of it any more than a person who takes a bus back and forth to school every day can drive one on their own. Two studies conducted by the Stanford History Education Group in 2016 and 2019 confirmed that students in middle school through college struggle with evaluating the veracity of information they encounter online.[2]

Although more people are recognizing that facility with a device does not equate to facility with discerning whether information is credible, there remains a belief that students "just know" how to research. Access to devices and broadband has only exacerbated this mentality—type any search string into Google, and a user is bound to get results. Unfortunately, many searchers conflate receiving results with receiving access to credible information. In summarizing Michael Lynch's book *The Internet of Us* in their 2020 article "Can Middle Schoolers Learn to Read the Web Like Experts? Possibilities and

Limits of a Strategy-Based Intervention," Kohnen, Mertens, and Boehm state, "The easier it is to access information, Lynch posited, the more likely we are to treat it as automatically credible, much as we instinctively trust information acquired through our senses."[3] It is essential that K–12 students have regular exposure to information literacy lessons so that they develop the skills to become critical consumers and producers of information.

THE FLEXIBILITY FACTOR

Many middle school students arrive at their new school having never experienced a library research project. They may have experienced research projects that were done in the classroom under the guidance of their teacher. If they were lucky enough to have a full-time school librarian at their elementary school, they may have had the opportunity to receive information literacy-related lessons on topics such as basic database searching, the utilization of print and digital nonfiction books, and how to cite their sources. If the elementary library program was not flexibly scheduled and the school librarian and classroom teacher were not able to collaborate, then chances are that many of the information literacy lessons occurred in isolation, making the transfer of knowledge to future research experiences difficult.

Middle school library programs tend to be flexibly scheduled, meaning that school librarians work collaboratively with the subject area teachers at the point of need, rather than seeing a set roster of students weekly, and typically without the classroom teacher. A flexibly scheduled program provides opportunities for sustained research experiences, where students can conduct research under the guidance of their school librarians and subject area teachers over the course of multiple days, even weeks, as the projects become more rigorous. In this collaborative environment, it is helpful to think of the subject area teacher as the content expert and the school librarian as the information literacy expert. Certified school library media specialists have taken graduate-level coursework on how to teach information literacy.

Research experiences created collaboratively should address objectives from both the teachers' and the librarians' curricula. Information literacy skills are necessary for all areas of life, and, ideally, classes from all core content areas in all grades visit the library for research experiences so students can recognize and experience different connections. Having students visit the library with a variety of different classes also allows for scaffolding of research skills and opportunities for reinforcement.

CURRICULUM IS KEY

Like other subject areas, school library programs should have a current, board-approved curriculum. A school library program's curriculum should be

Beth Thomas

rooted in the national standards, which can be crosswalked with state learning standards. The American Association of School Librarians (AASL)[4] already provides crosswalks with the Next Generation Science Standards, the International Society for Technology in Education (ISTE)[5] Standards for Students and Educators, the Future Ready Framework, Google's CS (Computer Science) First Curriculum,[6] and The Association for Supervision and Curriculum Development (ASCD)[7] Whole Child Tenets. Updating this curriculum should be part of a district's curriculum rewriting cycle, and administrators should be encouraged to include their school librarian in curriculum discussions in the content areas as well. When school librarians are aware of future units of study, they can plan ahead to curate or even order resources to support the updated curriculum.

The 2018 AASL Standards Framework for Learners connects to many aspects of information literacy: formulating questions for personal interest or a curricular project, seeking a variety of sources, questioning and assessing the validity and accuracy of information, organizing information, and ethically using information to create their end products.[8] As school librarians write curricula for their programs, they should include lessons on the various types of online sources:

> We recommend that curriculum be developed that teaches students to recognize the types of sources encountered online, including those listed above (news organizations, government agencies, etc.). Without building this background knowledge, we believe students will always be fighting against misinformation without a sense of how to combat it.[9]

As school librarians develop information literacy lessons, they should include instruction on the various types of sources their students will encounter as they research online.

IT IS A PROCESS

At its core, research is an iterative process, and reflection is an important component of that process. Students should be aware of the different steps involved in the research process—identifying an information need, thinking about what sources might help them locate the needed information, reading and taking notes from these sources, synthesizing their research into a cohesive end product, and evaluating both the final product and the process they experienced. Most importantly, students should understand that research is not linear.

Source curation is essential to help guide middle school students to use vetted sources. There are a variety of curation tools available for educators. My co-librarian and I utilize LibGuides, https://lcjsms.summit.libguides.com/, to curate resources for research projects. LibGuides[10] is a content management and curation platform. Librarians can include links to applicable subscription databases, and vetted websites, and can embed videos and upload documents. From the first time they visit the library until they are ready to graduate in eighth grade, our students know to go to LibGuides when they have a research project. We rarely set students loose on the free web—we want them to establish good searching and evaluation techniques as they progress from grade to grade. We include links to vetted websites and explain that this means a librarian or a teacher has looked through it first and determined that the information is accurate. Students are always guided to our subscription databases first. Modeling resources will hopefully help students develop good research habits: "It is easier to start with good examples of sources than to teach students to ferret out all of the bad."[11]

SIXTH GRADE

My co-librarian and I work with our content area colleagues to develop research experiences that combine our information literacy objectives with their curricular objectives. We work in partnership with our teachers when classes visit the library. Students learn that their teachers are subject area specialists and their librarians are research experts. Since there are two of us and we have two classroom areas, we are able to work with multiple classes at once.

Sixth graders' first research project is with their social studies class. The research focuses on the modern-day countries of the Fertile Crescent. Students are introduced to the Big 6 Research Model by teaching them the "Super Three"—plan, do, review.[12] The opening discussion question is, "Why is it important to follow a recipe when making a meal?" Students recognize that following a recipe ensures that they use the correct ingredients, measurements, temperature, etc., so that their meal comes out tasting and looking delicious and that no one falls victim to food poisoning or overcooked food. Research is just like following a recipe—it is a step-by-step process, and students are taught that when they are aware of the steps, they are better prepared to be successful with their research projects.

Students are introduced to our subscription databases and learn how to take notes utilizing the Cornell Note-taking method. In the Cornell method, there are columns for keywords, notes, page numbers if using a book, and spaces for citations and reflection. Pre-formatted notesheets (graphic organizers) are provided for them to use, and we explain that studies have shown that writing out notes rather than typing is better for learning and retaining information.[13] Figure 5.1 shows an example of the notesheet students use when reading database articles.

Your name:_____ Database Notesheet
Author, if provided (last name, first name) _____ , _____ .
Title of Source (article title) "_____."
Title of Container (name of database) _____.
Publisher, if provided _____, Publication date, if provided _____.
Location (url ex. www.xyz.com) _____. Date Accessed (today) _____.
Month/Day/Year

Keyword	Notes (do not copy full sentences)

Your own thoughts, reflections, ideas

Figure 5.1 Cornell Note sheet. *Source*: Beth Thomas.

Students are introduced to MLA citation style and learn that our subscription databases provide information that is written by professionals and edited to ensure accuracy. They learn to identify keywords in the project guidelines created by their teachers, and we explain that their notes should be bulleted and in "caveman language." Cavemen did not speak in full sentences, and we explain that if students read their notes out loud, they should sound like a caveman. If it sounds like they are reading from an article or a book, did they copy word-for-word? If they plagiarize during the note-taking process it will be very difficult for them to avoid plagiarism when using their notes to create their end product. We also explain that if they find it impossible to pull out pertinent information from a source and put it in caveman language, they may need to find a different source that they can better comprehend. Students are taught that it is important for researchers to use multiple sources and are introduced to our EBSCO K-8 eBook collection, print books, our other subscription databases, and vetted websites.[14]

Later in the year, sixth graders visit with their science classes for an ecosystems/endangered species research project. We reinforce using our academic databases and introduce them to lateral reading with an activity involving the hoax site for the "Pacific Northwest Tree Octopus," https://zapatopi.net/treeoctopus/. Rather than just scrolling up and down the website vertically, they open up new tabs and search for the author or organization responsible for a website and/or information included within the site.[15] Students answer some basic questions about the site and then select one of three topics mentioned on the site: Lyle Zapato (creator of the site), Kelvinic University (university that Mr. Zapato said he attended), and Republic of Cascadia, the purported habitat/range of the Tree Octopus. Students search one of those topics in World Book, EBSCO's Middle Search Plus database, and Google. After encountering zero results in the databases, it quickly becomes apparent through the Google search that this is a hoax site and the Tree Octopus does not exist. We use this opportunity to emphasize that researchers should use multiple resources and if they find a website through a search engine, they need to look deeper at who is providing the information.

SEVENTH GRADE

In seventh grade, students create accounts in NoodleTools, https://www.noodletools.com, a citation management platform. They practice using it with their science classes and are required to cite a book, database, and a website. They also receive a lesson on plagiarism with their language arts class. Lycoming College has a fun plagiarism video game that the students love to play: https://www.lycoming.edu/library/plagiarism-game/. There are some more advanced concepts in the game that we cover during the lesson and, with some guidance, students are able to successfully beat the game.

Since students utilize images and video in their multimedia projects, we do a lesson on copyright. Students are instructed to cite any images, music, or video they use, and the lesson covers the four factors of fair use. All of our subscription databases have image galleries, and we emphasize that the images in the databases are accurate, appropriate, copyright-friendly, and they provide the citation! There are current real-life examples of copyright infringement (especially with musicians), and these cautionary tales capture our middle-schoolers' attention.

Another lesson that captures student attention is our web crawling/how a search engine works activity. We start the lesson by asking the students how many have used Google in the past:

- Month
- Week
- Twenty-four hours

The responses tend to be unanimous: almost everyone has used it in the past twenty-four hours. With Google being the first stop for most information-seekers, it is important that users understand how the search engine works: "Strategy and skills-based information literacy instruction holds promise but must be paired with foundational knowledge about how the internet is structured and the kinds of online sources."[16] For this activity, we tell students to suspend reality for a period. They are not students; they are web crawlers, software that is programmed to go out into the web and collect information from websites. I am not the librarian; I am the search engine, and the library is cyberspace. Hidden all throughout "cyberspace" are laminated tags that contain information that web crawling software collects from websites. Students literally crawl around the library, collecting tags, and then we reconvene and ask questions about what kinds of information they see on the tab (keywords, name of site, URL, etc.). We make sure some of the tags are in different languages to drive home the concept of the *world* wide web, and we also make sure that they do not have enough time to collect all the tags. This is because when someone is using a search engine, like Google, they are not searching the entirety of the internet. I then collect all of the tags and pretend to organize and index them. After they do the crawling exercise, we reinforce the physical activity with a slideshow that includes a video from Google about how a Google search works: https://www.youtube.com/watch?v=0eKVizvYSUQ.

In seventh grade, we also teach students about the concept of identifying strong keywords. They come to the library for research on alternative energy sources. Using the modeling technique, the librarian shows examples—keywords that could apply to any of the topics: benefi* (truncation is a skill we are able to teach via the keyword lesson), drawback*, advantag*, disadvantag*, etc. The guiding question for this activity is, "If you combine this keyword with your topic (hydropower, nuclear power, solar power), will you be able to get more pertinent articles?" We also advise students to include proper nouns such as names of organizations, laws, and locations. Just like research is an iterative process, reading, identifying and using different keywords, and searching are iterative. We have students keep track of their keywords in a Google Doc we share as a template via the teacher's Google Classroom so we can look at each student's efforts and schedule mini-lessons if they struggle.

We also introduce search limiters during this research experience. Our state library provides access to K–12-level EBSCO databases—and this is a perfect resource to use for both keyword searching practice and the use of limiters. We teach our students to always select the full-text limiter so they are provided with full articles, and they also learn that they can limit their results by publication date range, source type, cover story, etc.

EIGHTH GRADE

In eighth grade, students practice their lateral reading skills with a project in their science classes about climate change. For this activity, students are provided with a link to the website globalwarming.org. Since many searchers use top-level domains (.org, .com, .edu, etc.) to judge website validity,[17] we always make sure to remind them that .org does not mean a reputable or unbiased organization is behind the website. We teach students how to search for information about a website by utilizing a special search syntax:

siteaddress **-site:**siteaddress
    ex. globalwarming.org -site:globalwarming.org
    Utilizing this search string will provide links to websites that reference the website, but the site itself will not appear in results. Students are also asked to research the first contributor listed on the site, Myron Ebell. Articles about him mention his involvement with the Competitive Enterprise Institute and The Heartland Institute. Students are then asked to research these organizations. An article that shows up in the results is *The Washington Post*'s "Anatomy of a Washington Dinner: Who Funds the Competitive Enterprise Institute?" Readers learn that fossil fuel firms and transportation companies (that transport fossil fuels like coal and oil) are big donors.

When it comes to websites from the free web, we typically provide links to vetted websites on LibGuides. We have conducted lessons on how to use the advanced search mode of Google for when students need to go beyond the sites we provide. With this lesson, we compare Boolean searching with ordering food in a restaurant—the more specific you are, the more likely you are to get exactly what you are looking for. If I walk into a pizzeria and say, "I am hungry and I want some food," who knows what I will be served? I need to be specific: my "and" or "must have" items are a slice of pizza and a salad. The "or" or "might have" is cola—either Coke or Pepsi is fine. However, I hate the taste of diet, so the "not have" in this scenario is Diet Coke or Diet Pepsi. When my order arrives, I expect to see a slice and a salad and a cola that is not diet. After this example, we pair students up and provide them with a laminated Boolean operator chart and two envelopes with scenarios taped to the front. Inside the envelopes are the keywords from the scenarios because they need to use keywords when doing a search. They place the keywords in the correct Boolean columns. After getting some practice with Boolean operators, I show them which fields in Google advanced search mode correspond with the Boolean operators. I also show them how they have already been conducting Boolean searches in our catalog and subscription databases. Students are reminded that if they encounter an unfamiliar website, they need to dig deeper and incorporate lateral reading to determine its validity.

In eighth-grade English/Language Arts (ELA), students research social issues. One of their library activities is to watch Eli Pariser's 2011 Ted Talk about filter bubbles. Although this Ted Talk was presented over a decade ago, they recognize that algorithms still impact the information they receive. At the end of the period, students are asked to reflect on what they have learned about filter bubbles and if they think things have improved or have gotten worse in the past twelve years: (figures 5.2, 5.3, and 5.4).

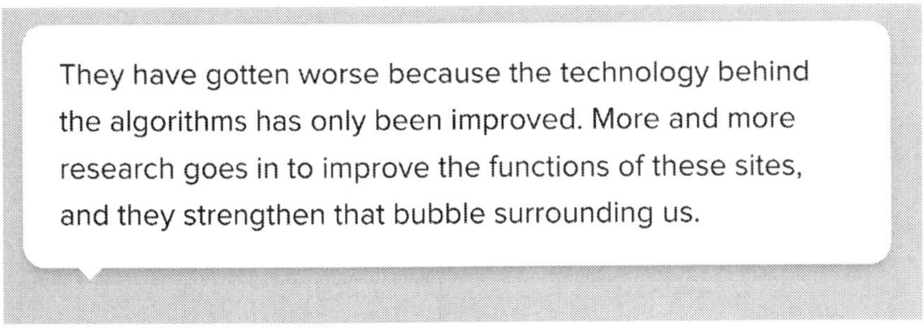

> They have gotten worse because the technology behind the algorithms has only been improved. More and more research goes in to improve the functions of these sites, and they strengthen that bubble surrounding us.

Figure 5.2 Eighth-Grade Student Response to Question about the Filter Bubble. *Source*: Beth Thomas.

> I think it has gotten worse. Technology has advanced greatly since then, and companies are so big and money hungry, they know filtering things you want to see will keep you engaged longer, making them money.

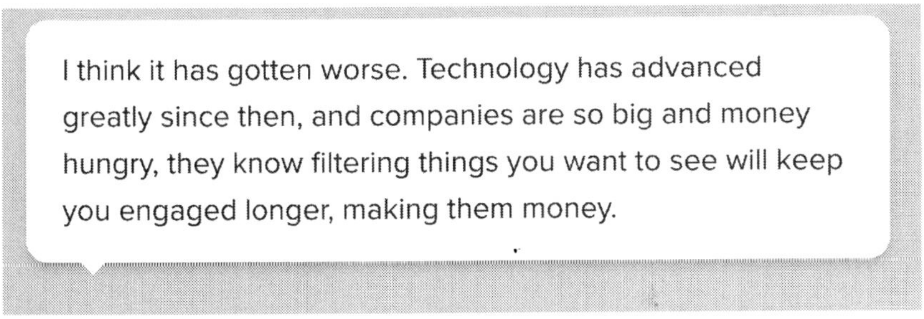

Figure 5.3 Eighth-Grade Student Response to Question about the Filter Bubble. *Source*: Beth Thomas.

> I think things have gotten worse, because if I use somebody else's device in my family, what I see is totally different. We really are living in bubbles, and basically we each have our own, personalized internet.

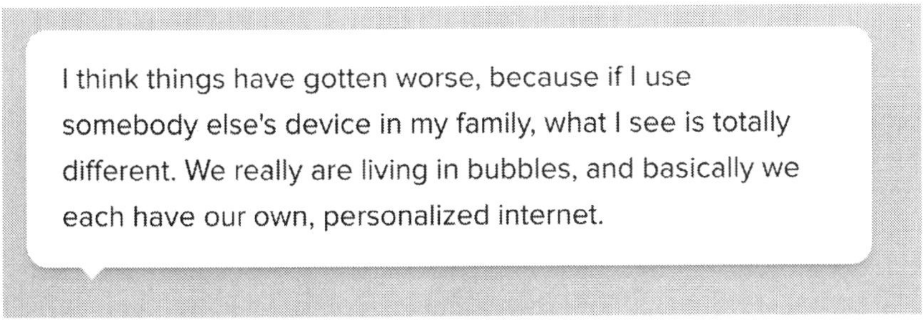

Figure 5.4 Eighth-Grade Student Response to Question about the Filter Bubble. *Source*: Beth Thomas.

The social injustice research project is a culminating experience for the eighth graders. It is an opportunity for them to put into practice the information literacy skills that they have learned over the past three years. It is also an opportunity to review The Big 6 research process. They learn that it is difficult to get started on their research if they do not have their task defined. We also require that they spend two periods in the library just reading and learning about their topic, which encompasses steps 2 and 3 of The Big 6—employing information-seeking strategies and locating and accessing sources. They start Step 4, using information, by reading and keeping track of strong keywords. However, they do not start to take notes until they have formulated a strong thesis statement. The ELA teachers work with them on this skill in the classroom before they come back to the library. Once they have an approved thesis statement, they start to take notes to support it and cite their sources in NoodleTools, continuing Step 4 of The Big 6. NoodleTools also offers digital notecards and outline tools, but the teachers we work with prefer to use it for citations only.

Students are required to use multiple types of sources for this project and are reminded that there is an EBSCO database search limiter that can help them get articles from specific types of sources like periodicals, book chapters, encyclopedia articles, etc. This is also an opportunity to highlight the other search limiters that can help them refine their search results, such as publication title, date range, and lexile level. Toward the end of their library time, students start to work on Step 5 of the Big 6, synthesis by organizing the information they have researched into an outline, which will prepare them to create their end product. The final step of the Big 6, evaluation, is a two-part process: evaluating the end product and evaluating the research process. Students fill in a Google Form to reflect on their research experience. Our hope is that this reflection will help prepare them for the rigors of high school and college-level research. We explain that they should continue utilizing the habits that helped them and break the habits that might have impeded them.

PREPARING FOR THE FUTURE

Middle school is a period of abundant change for students. They encounter more in-depth coursework and research projects. Many receive their first smartphones and create their own social media accounts. Information literacy instruction throughout middle school is essential in ensuring that students become discerning consumers and producers of information: "Middle school represents an opportune time for information literacy instruction from both a developmental and sociocultural perspective."[18] If students are to become college and career-ready informed citizens, it is imperative that K–12 schools provide an information literacy curriculum.

Beth Thomas

NOTES

1. Prensky, Marc. "Digital Natives, Digital Immigrants," *On the Horizon*, 9 (5), Last modified October 5, 2001. Accessed November 7, 2023. https://www.marcprensky.com/writing/Prensky%20-%20Digital%20Natives,%20Digital%20Immigrants%20-%20Part1.pdf.
2. Breakstone, Joel, Mark Smith, Sam Wineburg, Amie Rapaport, Jill Carle, Marshall Garland, and Anna Saavedra. "Students' Civic Online Reasoning: A National Portrait," *Stanford History Education Group*, November 14, 2019. Accessed November 7, 2023. https://stacks.stanford.edu/file/druid:gf151tb4868/Civic%20Online%20Reasoning%20National%20Portrait.pdf.
3. Kohnen, Angela, Gillian Mertens, and Shelby Boehm. "Can Middle Schoolers Learn to Read the Web Like Experts? Possibilities and Limits of a Strategy-Based Intervention," *Journal of Media Literacy Education*, 12 (2), 2020, 64–79. https://research.ebsco.com/linkprocessor/plink?id=da07541e-f6d3-3666-baa2-ed0fa52464f6.
4. American Library Association. American Association of School Librarians. Last modified 2023. Accessed December 12, 2023. https://www.ala.org/aasl/.
5. International Society for Technology in Education. ISTE. Last modified 2023. Accessed December 12, 2023. https://iste.org/.
6. "Embracing Students' Passions through Computer Science," Google CS First. Accessed December 15, 2023. https://csfirst.withgoogle.com/s/en/about.
7. ASCD. Last modified 2023. Accessed December 12, 2023. https://www.ascd.org/.
8. American Library Association. "AASL Standards Framework for Learners," American Association of School Librarians. Last modified February 5, 2018. Accessed November 7, 2023. https://standards.aasl.org/wp-content/uploads/2018/08/180206-AASL-framework-for-learners-2.pdf.
9. Kohnen, Mertens, and Boehm, "Can Middle Schoolers Learn to Read the Web Like Experts? Possibilities and Limits of a Strategy-Based Intervention," *Journal of Media Literacy Education*, 12 (2), 2020, 64–79. https://research.ebsco.com/linkprocessor/plink?id=da07541e-f6d3-3666-baa2-ed0fa52464f6.
10. "LibGuides & LibGuides CMS," SpringShare. Last modified 2023. Accessed December 15, 2023. https://springshare.com/libguides/.
11. Kohnen, Mertens, and Boehm, "Can Middle Schoolers Learn to Read the Web Like Experts? Possibilities and Limits of a Strategy-Based Intervention," *Journal of Media Literacy Education*, 12 (2), 2020, 64–79. https://research.ebsco.com/linkprocessor/plink?id=da07541e-f6d3-3666-baa2-ed0fa52464f6.
12. "What Is the Big6?," The Big 6. Accessed November 7, 2023. https://thebig6.org/thebig6andsuper3-2.
13. Askvik, Eva Ose, F. R. (Ruud) van der Weel, and Audrey L. H. van der Meer, "The Importance of Cursive Handwriting Over Typewriting for Learning in the Classroom: A High-Density EEG Study of 12-Year-Old Children and Young Adults," *Frontiers in Psychology*, 11, July 28, 2020. Accessed November 7, 2023. https://www.ncbi.nlm.nih.gov/pmc/articles/PMC7399101/.
14. Other databases we subscribe to include Britannica, CultureGrams, World Book, Infobase, Gale, FactCite, and Cavendish Square Digital. Recommended websites include the Library of Congress, Smithsonian, Reuters, NOAA, and so on.

15. "News Lit Tips: Expand Your View with Lateral Reading," News Literacy Project. Accessed November 7, 2023. https://newslit.org/tips-tools/expand-your-view-with-lateral-reading/.
16. Kohnen, Mertens, and Boehm. "Can Middle Schoolers Learn to Read the Web Like Experts? Possibilities and Limits of a Strategy-Based Intervention," *Journal of Media Literacy Education*, 12 (2), 2020, 64–79. https://research.ebsco.com/linkprocessor/plink?id=da07541e-f6d3-3666-baa2-ed0fa52464f6.
17. Breakstone, et al., "Students' Civic Online Reasoning: A National Portrait," *Stanford History Education Group*, November 14, 2019. Accessed November 7, 2023. https://stacks.stanford.edu/file/druid:gf151tb4868/Civic%20Online%20Reasoning%20National%20Portrait.pdf.
18. Kohnen, Mertens, and Boehm. "Can Middle Schoolers Learn to Read the Web Like Experts? Possibilities and Limits of a Strategy-Based Intervention," *Journal of Media Literacy Education*, 12 (2), 2020, 64–79. https://research.ebsco.com/linkprocessor/plink?id=da07541e-f6d3-3666-baa2-ed0fa52464f6.

6

Visual Literacy in the Age of AI

WHY IT MATTERS

Cathy Collins, Library Media Specialist, Sharon Public Schools, Massachusetts

I am fortunate to have been raised by an English teacher father who not only loved words and poetry but also art, and who was a successful, award-winning professional photographer. He trained my young eyes to seek beauty and my mind and heart to stop, and closely and lovingly observe objects in nature as well as people. He also taught me to read the light and color around me. Nature and museum outings were as much a part of my childhood as visits to bookstores.

Dave Gray, the founder of visual thinking company XPLANE, said,

> Three R's are no longer enough. Our world is changing fast—faster than we can keep up with through our historical modes of thinking and communicating. Visual literacy—the ability to both read and write visual information; the ability to learn visually; to think and solve problems in the visual domain, . . . is a requirement for success in business and in life.

The explicit teaching and assessment of Visual Literacy, an essential element of Digital Literacy, is frequently overlooked and/or undertaught within secondary classrooms. Visual Literacy affords learners the opportunity to connect with the world and each other, understanding their role and the role of others in everything that they view. However, there are many aspects of Visual Literacy that educators need to learn in order to effectively teach the topic.[1]

Approximately 3.2 billion images and 720,000 hours of video are shared online daily.[2] Given this flood of visual information, it's challenging for us, even as informed and educated adults, to analyze the meaning behind those images, and to determine what's real and what's not.

"Pictures are no longer precious; there are just too many of them," writes Jessi Hempel for *Fortune* Magazine.

Once collected and preserved as art, or to document memories, they are now emerging as a new language, one that promises to be both more universally understood and accessible to anyone. In the 1400s, Europeans were considered literate if they could spell their names—and 80% could not. Then came the printing press. Within a century, people could read and write in growing numbers, and the literate were able to express complex ideas in writing. This mass shift in literacy ushered in progress in science, general education, and the arts. We are now entering a similar period for images. Our smartphones and the Internet that enables them are the modern-day equivalent to movable type, and these tools are still very new.[3]

At the Toledo Museum of Art, Brian Kennedy has been conducting research to learn more about how visual literacy affects the way students think.
"Nearly 30% of the brain's cortex is devoted to visual processing," he said.

More than the other human senses. The optic nerve has over a million nerve fibers. Ninety percent of all the information we take in from the world we take in visually. With so much of the brain's cortex devoted to visual processing, it is logical that visual literacy is the key to sensory literacy.

He created a visual literacy curriculum, which involves training students to understand their own viewing process.
"Looking and seeing are the same thing, right? What is the difference between these two actions?" he said.

If visual literacy is the ability to read, write, and comprehend visual language, then looking at an image is similar to skimming a text while seeing an image is comparable to reading it. . . . As you begin to slow down and look closer, you will begin to make note of the different elements in the image. This is called observing—the process of building a catalog of visual elements—and is the bridge between looking and seeing.[4]

Our students need to master this type of thinking so that they can understand the way media affects them, along with the motivation behind the sharing of images.
"It's as important to be visually literate, to understand pictures and how they affect us, as it is to be word-literate," Kennedy said. "Many of us employ visual language, often without realizing it. Being fluent in the language of images gives us an advantage at school, at work, and at home."[5]

Though lip service is given to the importance of visual literacy, there is still, generally speaking, an underemphasis on it in the K–12 world across grade levels and subject areas. *New York Times* art critic Roberta Smith asserts that we need to place more emphasis on visual learning. While society expects us to develop a high level of verbal literacy, visual literacy and visual IQ are "essentially perceived as useless. 'We don't teach what I'd call visual literacy. We teach the other kind. I think it would be pretty amazing if art history were taught in public schools from an early age.'"[6]

Just as textual literacy cannot be restricted to the English classroom, visual and other new literacies cannot be limited to the arts classroom. Since much of our newest technologies are dominated by visuals, we would shortchange our students if we didn't help them think critically about the image-driven messages they receive on a daily basis. Moreover, we would fail them if we did not aid them in effectively and purposely creating their own image-driven messages.

Perhaps there is no more prominent advocate of new literacies than American filmmaker George Lucas, who insists in the Edutopia article, "Life on the Screen: Visual Literacy in Education," that all forms of communication skills thoroughly be taught.[7] He states:

Today we work with the written or spoken word as the primary form of communication. But we also need to understand the importance of graphics, music and cinema, which are just as powerful and in some ways more deeply intertwined with young people's culture. We live and work in a visually sophisticated world, so we must be sophisticated in using all the forms of communication, not just the written word.[8]

Ideally, all young people would have the same opportunity to immerse themselves in the world of art and photography. Regardless, we can employ certain strategies to provide all students with sound visual literacy skills that will serve them throughout their lives.

VISUAL LITERACY TEACHING STRATEGIES

Practice Visual Thinking Strategies

Visual thinking strategies encourage students to express their ideas and make meaning with words through the creation of their own visuals. The visuals can be hand-drawn with crayons, colored pencils, and/or markers, or digitally created using apps, programs and techniques such as Sketch Notes, Adobe Express, Canva, Google Drawings, etc. Basic visuals can be constructed in a few minutes at the end of a class as a survey of students' understanding of a topic, and can be used as a check for understanding, exit ticket, or formative in-class assignment.[9]

Visual Thinking Activities

- The 4 W's activity helps students make observations, connections, and inferences about the motivation behind images and to develop ideas about the significance of an image by asking "What do I see?" "What does it remind me of?" (Another image? A personal experience?) "What's the creator's purpose?" (to analyze, persuade, express, document, entertain?) "So what?" (Why does it matter? What is the significance?)
- Five Card Flickr: In Five Card Flickr, players are dealt five random photos. To promote visual literacy, have students follow these steps:

  1. Jot down one word that they associate with each image.
  2. Identify a song that comes to mind for one or more of the images.
  3. Describe what all the images have in common.
  4. Compare answers with classmates.

- During a subsequent discussion, ask students to show what elements of the photo prompted their responses.Image analysis worksheets: To promote analysis of key features specific to different formats, pick an appropriate tool from the National Archives:
  - Written Document Analysis Worksheet
  - Photo Analysis Worksheet: https://www.archives.gov/files/education/lessons/worksheets/photo_analysis_worksheet_former.pdf
  - Cartoon Analysis Worksheet https://www.archives.gov/files/education/lessons/worksheets/cartoon_analysis_worksheet_former.pdf
  - Poster Analysis Worksheet https://www.archives.gov/files/education/lessons/worksheets/poster_analysis_worksheet_former.pdf
  - Map Analysis Worksheet https://www.archives.gov/files/education/lessons/worksheets/map_analysis_worksheet_former.pdf
  - Artifact Analysis Worksheet https://www.archives.gov/files/education/lessons/worksheets/artifact_analysis_worksheet_former.pdf
  - Motion Picture Analysis Worksheet: https://www.archives.gov/files/education/lessons/worksheets/motion_picture_analysis_worksheet_former.pdf

Present Photos without Captions

I love using The New York Times "What's Going On In This Picture?" to give my media literacy students regular practice in analyzing images. I break them into groups and then we share our thoughts as a class. On Sundays from September to May, the site posts an intriguing photograph without its caption. I ask students to think critically about what they see. They need to answer the following questions:

- What's going on in this picture?
- What do you see that makes you say that?
- What more can you find?
- What do you see that makes you say that?
- What more can you find?

Teach Graphic Design, Multimedia Production, and Coding Alongside Poetry and Writing

At the middle school level, I integrate an Hour of Code broadcast news activity in which my students create their own video newscasts, including layout and graphics, through coding, and run a fun "Code Your Own Poem" activity in which they add graphics and sound through coding to match the tone and mood of selected poems. My students have also created videos to illustrate their reimagined versions of news stories based on nursery rhymes and fairy tales. At the high school level, I've collaborated with teachers to help students bring their poems to life through video and digital music tools. All of this cross-disciplinary, multimedia activity helps young creators to think out of the box and to become comfortable using a wide range of technology tools and 4 C's skills as they develop important visual literacy competencies.

Creativity, communication, collaboration, and critical thinking are widely acknowledged as the new foundational skills. With the 4 C's, students learn how to analyze problems and to think outside of the box. They work in partnership with others to problem-solve. And they learn to look at new ways of applying technology to assist them in the creative process.

Think of Visuals as More Than Just "Visual Aids"; Don't Discriminate against Graphic Novels, Comics, and Manga

Visual material is more than just a supplementary form of communication. Comic books and graphic novels are highly engaging to many of our students and no less worthy of their time and attention than other books. Integrate them across subject areas and watch your student engagement level rise.

Teach Infographics

Infographics are an excellent tool for students to share what they understand about a topic and to connect vocabulary, data and other information. Infographics are being used increasingly across media platforms as a way to wedge large quantities of information into small, visually appealing, interactive spaces. Infographics are a great way for students to "show what they know." For students, creating an infographic can connect classroom concepts to real-world data and examples that they research and analyze. As a visual representation of data, students are combining informational, visual, and digital literacies as they create. Infographics are also excellent for use as media analysis examples, as data and other content in infographics are as easily manipulated and prone to bias as other content.

We Are All Visual Learners

Researchers at Georgetown University Medical Center's Department of Neuroscience found that we learn to read by adding words to our "visual dictionary." The mother of an American friend of mine shared that she knew she had finally mastered the German language after a trip to the movies with a friend in the German town where she had moved. Though she thought the movie had been in English, her friend shared the next day that it had actually been in German. My friend's Mom, Terry, had an epiphany at that moment, realizing that she had stopped verbally translating from English to German in her head. Likewise, "The sooner teachers abandon the dusty old Learning Styles Theory and realize we all learn visually, the sooner our students will be empowered to become visually literate."[10]

Give Students Practice Representing Ideas without Words

"Visual communication deserves much more respect than it is given, and can serve education in so many ways that the written word can't. Let's work to appreciate this."[11] I encourage my students to "sketchnote" rather than use just text for note-taking. Sketchnotes are visual notes created from a mix of handwriting, drawings, hand-lettering, shapes, and visual elements like arrows, boxes, and lines. They don't require special drawing skills, but instead require students to listen well in order to visually synthesize and summarize ideas by using a combination of writing and drawing. Here is one example of what sketchnotes can look like: (see figure 6.1).

Expose Students to the Metaverse

The metaverse is the next evolution of the internet—and it is bringing new worlds to life for our students. It spans a range of technologies, including virtual reality headsets that can transport our students to whole new environments, immerse them in virtual spaces where they and others can interact as avatars; as well as augmented reality glasses that will one day project computer-generated images onto the world around us; and mixed reality experiences that blend both physical and virtual environments. These technologies create a more immersive, 3-D visual and sensory experience where students can feel like they are right there with another person or in another place.

Teach Students to Study and Create Editorial Cartoons

The process of studying and creating editorial cartoons sharpens visual literacy skills and can bring clarity and a deeper level of understanding to history topics. It can also help students process emotionally troubling current events as a form of art therapy.

Figure 6.1 Sketchnote Example. *Source*: Kimberly Zajac.

Teach Critical Thinking through Visuals with AI Image Generators

Here are some suggested learning activities that use AI image generators:

- **Add illustrations to a story.** Have students use their imaginations to ask an AI image generator to create illustrations that the illustrator of the story didn't create, or to invent new ones.
- **Create an alternate ending.** What if a character in a story chose a different path? What if someone in history did something different, or we had students recreate a historical photo to include one new element that changed world events?
- **Assign an illustrated writing prompt.** Create an image of a person, a place, an event, etc. Then let students write about it.
- **Illustrate a story problem.** Generate an image with AI that shows students what a story problem might look like to create more clarity, or assess their level of understanding through AI images they create.
- **Create an image or diagram to describe.** This could easily be applied in world language classrooms or science classrooms. Generate images that students then use grammar, vocabulary, or new concepts to describe.
- **Create images of people to add dialogue.** What would historical characters say to each other or to us as citizens of a future world? Could students

envision a dialogue between themselves and the characters in a story? Students could use AI image generators to create images for comics or a storyboard, adding speech/thought bubbles and captions.[12]

Seeing Is Not Always Believing: Helping Students Sort Real from Manipulated Images

Every day misinformation is created and spread online. While the topics may change from day to day, the methods of manipulation have mostly stayed the same. Images and media are presented out of context, photos and videos are digitally manipulated and all sorts of fabricated claims gain traction simply because they're attributed to a credible source.[13]

We can help our students learn to push back against visual misinformation by teaching them that seeing is not always believing, and by providing them with the skills they need to become information-savvy.

Here are three ways to counter common tactics being used to spread misinformation online these days:

1. **Recognizing genuine imagery presented out of context:** Nearly every image and video that we come across on social media is presented to us alongside a piece of text. This format is very easy to manipulate. Our students need to know that bad actors, or people posting with the intention to deceive, can quickly and easily use genuine images out of context to create a convincing piece of misinformation.

2. **Recognizing manipulated images:** Manipulated media can be just as deceptive as out-of-context media. Altered photos and videos often appear genuine at first glance, especially when the edits are subtle. But altering the visuals tends to leave behind cues that careful observers are likely to catch. With generative AI tools that can alter a person's movements and mimic their voices, bad actors can make it seem as if prominent people such as politicians are making statements that they never did. Digital editing tools have made it difficult to distinguish between genuine and doctored content. But we can teach our students that by looking at the surrounding context of a piece of media we can still sometimes discover important clues about authenticity.

3. **Identifying impostors:** Impostor content works by presenting false information as if coming from a reputable, reliable source. By presenting a fabricated news report as coming from a reputable source, bad actors cannot only make a fictitious item seem plausible but they can also disparage credible news outlets and exacerbate distrust in credible news sources. Fabricating social media posts is another popular form of impostor content. Both fake news headlines and fabricated posts tend to circulate solely in the form of a screenshot, which is a red flag to watch out for.[14]

Cathy Collins

When we teach our students about the tactics that these bad actors use, we increase their ability to spot that content and avoid being duped or spreading misinformation.

DIGITAL VERIFICATION: CONCLUSION

We can teach our students how to do reverse image Google searches and conduct lateral reading across platforms to determine the original source of an image. The News Literacy Project has excellent tutorials and related lessons on those important visual and news literacy skills. But before we get to that step, there are some simple questions that can help our students ask themselves to potentially figure out whether a photo or video on social media is fake:

- Was it originally made for social media?
- How widely and for how long was it circulated and by whom?
- What responses did it receive?
- Who were the intended audiences?

Often enough, the logical conclusions they derive from the answers will be enough to help them weed out inauthentic visuals and related content.[15]

NOTES

1. Turner, John, "The Difference between Digital Learning and Digital Literacy? A Practical Perspective," 2012.https://jturner56.files.wordpress.com/2013/01/digital-literacy-paper.pdf.
2. Thomson, T. J., Daniel Angus, and Paula Dootson, "3.2 Billion Images and 720,000 Hours of Video Are Shared Online Daily. Can You Sort Real from Fake?" *The Conversation*, November 2, 2020. Accessed December 5, 2023. https://theconversation.com/us.
3. "Why Visual Literacy Is More Important than Ever & 5 Ways to Cultivate It," Open Colleges, 2015. https://www.opencolleges.edu.au/blogs/articles/why-visual-literacy-is-more-important-than-ever-5-ways-to-cultivate-it.
4. Ibid.
5. Ibid.
6. Ibid.
7. James Daly, "Life on the Screen: Visual Literacy in Education," *Edutopia, George Lucas Educational Foundation*, September 14, 2004. https://www.edutopia.org/life-screen.
8. Ayotte, Lori, and Cathy Collins, "Using Short Videos to Enhance Reading and Writing in the ELA Curriculum," *The English Journal*, 106, no. 3 (2017): 19–24. http://www.jstor.org/stable/26359281.

9. Finley, Todd, "Common Core in Action: 10 Visual Literacy Strategies," *Edutopia*. *George Lucas Educational Foundation*, February 19, 2014. https://www.edutopia.org /blog/ccia-10-visual-literacy-strategies-todd-finley.
10. Ibid.
11. Ibid.
12. Miller, Matt, "AI Image Generators: 10 Tools, 10 Classroom Uses," *Ditch That Textbook*, September 12, 2023. https://ditchthattextbook.com/ai-image-generators/.
13. Strauss, Valerie, "Perspective | Top Trending Misinformation Tactics Everyone Can Learn to Spot." *The Washington Post*, November 16, 2023. https://www.washingtonpost.com/education/2023/11/16/top-trending-misinformation-tactics/.
14. Ibid.
15. Thomson, Angus, and Dootson, "3.2 Billion Images and 720,000 Hours of Video Are Shared Online Daily. Can You Sort Real from Fake?" *The Conversation*, November 2, 2020. Accessed December 5, 2023. https://theconversation.com/us.

7

Teaching Tech Literacy from Toddlers to Tweens

Tricina Strong-Beebe, School Library Media Specialist, Hainesport Township School District, New Jersey and Adjunct Professor, PennWest-Clarion University, Pennsylvania

CREATING AN INFORMATION LITERACY ROADMAP WITH TECHNOLOGY

Every young learner is exposed to technology at some point in their early years. Whether kids are exploring their curiosity or just mimicking adult behavior, screen time seems to be an inevitable part of modern childhood. However, the reality is that despite all we know about the physical and mental health risks associated with excessive screen time, parents and educators receive little instruction on how to navigate and manage technology use among children.

Consider all the safety features that come with infant furniture, toys, and accessories. From car seats and strollers to swings and saucers, baby and toddler products are highly regulated for safety in the United States. Parents and caregivers have the tools and resources to provide a safe and secure environment for their infants and toddlers. In contrast, there are far fewer guidelines and restrictions for technology to keep children safe online.

INEQUITIES OF TECHNOLOGY

Technology use is far from equitable for children throughout the U.S. Devices come in many shapes, sizes, and price points. Children may not have ready access to high-quality, reliable devices or fast and dependable Wi-Fi service in their communities. Lack of telecommunication towers creates a barrier preventing connectivity in underserved and remote locations. Socioeconomics can also play a large part in separating the haves and the have-nots.

The quality of students' devices impacts their ability to retrieve digital information. Storage capacity, network bandwidth, signal strength, and speed all impact if and how they access online content. A slower operating system or limited applications can significantly hinder a child's digital experience. Other devices may offer supportive extensions that raise the bar for early learners, like a "reader app," text available as dyslexia font, or paid assistive applications that can aid with advanced learning and diverse needs. Equity is not only determined by logistics; it is a reflection of a child's home environment, support network, and socioeconomic status.

The problem can be especially apparent for English learners in small and rural school districts that lack the resources to employ translators. As a result, translating documents like lesson plans, homework, and emails can take longer. Some families simply place greater emphasis on incorporating technology into everyday life, while others have more reservations about encouraging screen time in the home. Yet despite these glaring inequities, school districts and government funding have made it essential for all students to work from a level playing field when it comes to technology. But with so many variables at play, that goal can seem nearly impossible. Finding the right relationship with technology in the early years is important. Yet, questions still remain:

What is the right amount of technology?

Who determines the relationship a child has with technology in the early years?

How do we communicate this information with families, students, and schools?

The answers to these questions can be found in your nearest library or with the help of a certified school librarian. Libraries can be "game changers" when it comes to closing the digital divide and offering access to digital literacy training and support. Librarians assist with developing applications and content that encourage self-sufficiency, balance, participation, and partnership. Library specialists can create a vibrant community gathering center with robust broadband Wi-Fi service, high-quality tech support, lesson plans, and guidance. Many public libraries have lending stations providing complimentary computer devices to borrow as needed and resources to receive discounted broadband service for underserved communities. School librarians can be the most advantageous educators when it comes to inequities in education. Media specialists can assist with locating verifiable websites, share grade-appropriate learning resources, and curate material that can aid in the provision of various tools for students and staff.

It is important to know your learner. School librarians have an incredible advantage when it comes to understanding student development and needs, as they see every student in the building at every grade level. School librarians follow students throughout their educational journey as their interests and needs evolve. They can often be the primary decision-makers for determining appropriate resources for each student, classroom, grade level, school, and district.

AUTOMATICITY WITH TECH LITERACY

Let's face it, we are continually barraged with information coming from all directions. Children today are exposed to a plethora of media sources—many of which lack sufficient filters. As parents and educators, we are tasked with developing strategies to empower children to sift through content, evaluate the quality of materials, and share information as an automated response. Creating automaticity for young learners is one key to producing emerging technology users for the twenty-first century. Creating an ingrained habit of purposeful assessment, evaluation, management, and sharing of information through a technology-driven platform is something that should be nurtured even at a young age. Teaching students early on the basics of acceptable consumption, creation, and communication through technology helps instill a simple, low-level response to accessing appropriate material. In time, this helps them adopt healthy habits for seeking and sharing digital information.

BABY STEPS: THE EARLY YEARS (PRESCHOOL-KINDERGARTEN)

Independent use of technology typically begins during the Pre-K and kindergarten years. Young minds start the process of evaluating the accuracy of what they are seeing, hearing, and reading. Navigating information overload and the ability to identify real and "fake" news are critical skills every student needs as they wade through the vast ocean of content available online.

Since technology is embedded in almost everything we do, parents and caregivers should establish clear and specific parameters to ensure engagement is developmentally appropriate.

Techniques for evaluating online informational resources should be implemented as soon as a child begins navigating technology under the supervision of a parent, caregiver, or teacher. Starting there, the child can continue building upon these basic skills to acquire information discernment as they grow to become a lifelong learner.

At this stage of development, childlike minds may be sparked by their imagination, creative narratives, and a false reality. This is the ideal time to ask questions about what is "real" using literature, playtime, television, and the internet as tools. Children will largely benefit from developing basic evaluation skills that require inquiry and an outcome for supportive evidence, answers to the *hows* and *whys,* and critical analysis through testimonial proof. Identifying what is *real* is the first step to applying information literacy to everyday life skills. Oftentimes, this skill set is reinforced through library lessons in which students learn to separate fact from fiction.

EARLY EVALUATION TOOLS IN A HIGH-TECH WORLD

Here are some tools and techniques to help students gain the skill of discernment when evaluating digital content.

Fact from Fiction

Library Science and English Language Arts curricula generally include instruction on identifying literature as fiction or nonfiction. Through this exercise, students learn the first steps of critical thinking and evaluation. For instance, when reading a storybook, they may wonder, *can animals talk? Is what I'm reading or hearing real or imaginary?* Educators may ask the student to give examples of how this is accurate and valid information. They may ask the child: *How can you PROVE this is real? What evidence makes you think this isn't accurate?*

At this age, these basic research strategies can be combined with real-world experience and fact-checking information to assess the validity of online information.

Credentials

Monitoring online resources is critical in the early stages of development. Introducing safe websites verified to be age-based and appropriate is a task for parents and educators alike. It's important to emphasize that students should stick to familiar apps and sites that have been approved by a trusted adult. Encouraging children to ask before exploring the web is another component of healthy online behavior. School librarians can help curate resources and materials for schools that would be best suited for families and classrooms.

Timed or Limited Usage

Screen time management is essential for every age and stage of development. Just as young children are taught the benefits of brushing their teeth and washing their hands, students should perceive balancing screen time as another healthy choice they make every day. Research[1] shows that excessive tech use contributes to a sedentary lifestyle, which increases the risk of many serious (and preventable) problems.

A moving body is necessary for optimal health and wellness, and it is possible to integrate technology in ways that promote physical activity. There are many fun and engaging digital apps and tools available to encourage movement in school and at home. Finding games that get kids up and active can help prevent conditions like obesity, cardiovascular disease, and diabetes, which can worsen with age and result in long-term health complications. Some examples include the use of Dash and Finch robots for both coding skills and movement. Integrating robotics with other content areas, such as physical education, science, art, and music, can also center hands-on learning while in motion.

GRADES: CONNECTING TO CONTENT

Whether through their school district, at home, playing with friends, or during everyday interactions, technology plays a large role in early education and development. Parents, caregivers, teachers, and educational support professionals have the task of supporting students as they explore technology and utilize and evaluate the information they receive. Conversations about media interactions are often the best way to start a positive dialogue about the benefits, risks, and alternatives of using technology.

Many schools provide opportunities for students to use devices independently prior to third grade. Some schools provide a one-to-one program, where they distribute one computer or tablet to every student, allowing access that is considered appropriate for grade-level usage. Unfortunately, classroom teachers are often so occupied with teaching the required content throughout the year that they have limited time to discuss the "dos and don'ts" regarding healthy tech consumption. Digital safety and responsibility are often overlooked simply because of time and resource constraints.

The critical thinking techniques children acquire in their earlier years can be invaluable for vetting news and other information. These students will produce the content of tomorrow. How they receive content is just as important as how they choose to share it with the public. Helping students understand the information highway is a long, winding journey filled with potholes and rest stops.

MUSCLE MEMORY

At this age and grade level, repetitive behaviors such as accessing applications, inputting computer commands, and understanding keyboard letter and symbol functions help students develop muscle memory in literacy. Incorporating positive repetitive technological practice can also support the advancement of implicit memory. Students can acquire various motor, memory, and technology proficiencies that broaden their scope of advanced technology interactions now and in the future.

Students who master basic muscle memory for computer usage at a young age may fare better when it comes to interactive multimedia and computer simulation. Students who lack automaticity and muscle memory may find themselves at a disadvantage when it comes to timed tests. Repetitive behaviors like logging on and off a computer, using mouse and keypad features, verifying websites, and applying "netiquette" adeptness for skill retention are vital skills for lifelong tech use. Students can engage in these automatic activities without a conscious effort as they begin acquiring more advanced skills over time. Rhyming, stories, songs, and games can be used to reinforce memory and encourage positive online interaction.

CONSISTENCY IS KEY

When using a roadmap for everyday travel, we can predict the quickest route, select roads without tolls, and even avoid accidents and traffic delays. Roadmaps for technology literacy are just as useful. Schools and districts can formulate a "go-to" roadmap designed to reflect their students' needs and goals.

At a young age, students will realize there is an initial process when turning on their devices, just like starting their ignition. This is where consistency comes in. Once students power up their devices, they are ready to incorporate those past lessons on how to safely explore the many routes of the world wide web. Technology literacy assists students in traversing their own unique paths filled with opportunities for detours, analysis, evaluation, and critical thinking[2] that eventually lead them to their final destination: a creative outlet for sharing what they learned.

ASSISTIVE TECHNOLOGY TOOLBOX

Assistive technology[3] ranges from simple, low-tech settings that adjust font size, to sophisticated computerized devices that speak to students. These innovative technologies allow students the same opportunities as their peers, and many are free or low-cost for public school use. School librarians, educators, and staff can help support students with additional needs by finding the best adaptive tool for learning. These programs and features can be used to support sensory and fine motor skills. Noise-blocking headphones, finger-grip options, a roller-ball mouse, touchpads with enhanced mobility, screen magnification, and other high-contrast displays are just a few features that help improve student functionality.

Another way to engage children with different needs is to offer a student-centered virtual "choice board" of educational games and technology. This is an easy and fun way to steer students toward properly vetted material for their age and ability. Choice boards can be interactive and designed to offer differentiation for various needs. Sometimes a teacher or school librarian can create adaptive choice boards to serve a broad range of specific student needs. They may incorporate audiobooks, app readers, or voice notes into daily lessons to increase interest and engagement.

Tricina Strong-Beebe

Knowing your students' strengths and needs will help you determine the best fit. Consider devices that are comfortable, lightweight, and durable. Some have padding, built-in straps for carrying, and large keyboards for better visibility.

CREATING HEALTHY HABITS

Just as a plate of cookies or a jar of candy can be tempting for any toddler to touch, taste, or take, we must be cognizant of the temptations that come with device and computer usage. Students at this age are more likely to push boundaries without proper discipline and an understanding of time management. Like eating too many cookies, the same is true for tech time: everything is best in moderation. In these early stages, it benefits students to understand the implications of both physical and mental health when it comes to over-usage of online time.

Many lesson plans discuss media balance and behavior that can be curtailed to this age group. Having consistent discussions regarding timed or limited usage will be imperative for students to understand the pitfalls of overuse on their minds and bodies. Timers, built-in applications, and other tools can help curtail tech use. Positive and motivating sites should be encouraged. Conversely, addictive and consuming material may be difficult for this age range to monitor or process. Teaching kids about proper time management is an ongoing process.

TECHNOLOGY AS AN INTELLIGENCE (THIRD-FIFTH GRADE)

With the ongoing need for online access to complete schoolwork, it's no wonder students in the upper elementary grade levels can't seem to escape screen time. Librarians can work together with classroom teachers and support staff to create "unplugged" activities for students.

Discussing how to best accommodate students' needs is vital. Paper copies of assignments, class discussions about "screen time," and reinforcement at home can help students acquire healthy relationships with technology. "Unplugged" lessons give students opportunities to develop and showcase their understanding of coursework. They also give the brain a rest from overstimulation online.

With an increase in computer usage at this stage, students may need help addressing ergonomics in school and at home. Proper posture, taking brain breaks, establishing an appropriate workspace, and being cognizant of exercise can aid in personal health and cognition. Age-appropriate resources can enable growth and development when selected strategically. Educators and school librarians are tasked with choosing from the multitude of online gaming and educational resources for students.

MEETING STUDENTS WHERE THEY ARE, AND ELEVATING STUDENTS IN NEED

Learning is not a one-size-fits-all process. As discussed earlier, children have different resources, intelligence, adaptability, and aptitude compared with their peers. When creating a digital roadmap, it is imperative to utilize everything within the technology toolbox to provide every child with the opportunity to access content. Ensuring accessibility will help offset the digital divide and ensure students stay on a level playing field with neighboring school districts and students across the globe. We want to prepare students to be equally technologically proficient when it comes to computerized testing and other digital-based learning applications and assessments.

SCHOOL AND PUBLIC LIBRARIES: A PERFECT PARTNERSHIP

When school librarians partner with local public libraries, they can tap into the wealth of resources available outside their school. The public library can often supplement material for school librarians and fill the gap with rich resources that may not be available in each school system. Also, a school librarian can advocate to their public or state library to ensure adequate technology tools are available for students at the local and state levels.

NOTES

1. Mitchell, Jonathan, "Physical Inactivity in Childhood from Preschool to Adolescence," *ACSM's Health & Fitness Journal*, 23, no. 5 (2019): 21. https://doi.org/10.1249/fit.0000000000000507.
2. Kharbach, Med, "The 8 Elements of Critical Thinking," *Educators Technology*, Last update May 5, 2024. https://www.educatorstechnology.com/2023/05/the-8-elements-of-critical-thinking.html.
3. Simon Technology Center, "Examples of Assistive Technology for Young Children," Technology to Improve Kids' Educational Success (TIKES), PACER Center, Minneapolis, MN. https://www.pacer.org/stc/pubs/STC-29.pdf.

8

Shifting Our Thinking from "Digital Natives" to "Digital Learners"

THE MYTH OF "DIGITAL NATIVES"

Steve Tetreault, School Library Media Specialist and William R. Satz Middle School, New Jersey

Too often, adults—and educators particularly—assume that the modern student is a "digital native." This term, coined by Marc Prensky, implies that children born in the past forty years grew up surrounded by the trappings of the "Digital Age," and are therefore completely acclimated to a technological world. It further implies that students understand and can successfully navigate technology without a need for instruction.

Unfortunately, this is an erroneous belief. No matter what the task, humans are more likely to understand more and perform at a higher level when they receive knowledge, context, and training. This is true of sports, of arts, of sciences—and of technology.

It is a grave mistake to presume that students either know about digital tools and resources or that they can "figure it out" because they seem adept at navigating certain applications or online environments. The fact of the matter is, if students do not receive explicit instruction in digital literacy, they are relying on whatever they can pick up informally. This usually leaves students without an understanding of what's beyond the surface of their understanding—why an app works the way it does, how it functions within the larger digital landscape, and rather critically, what information about users is being gathered along the way.

As educators, we want to encourage literacy in our students. To my mind, "literacy" is a term that encompasses the skills and knowledge needed to successfully navigate a topic. We regularly encourage math literacy, science literacy, and language literacy. But too often, we neglect literacies that are not traditionally seen as part of the broader public school curricula—especially when we ourselves may not have gotten direct instruction in one of those areas. Technological literacy is one such area.

Certainly, students have received limited computer instruction for many years. However, this has tended to be an elective class rather than a core class. Reaching far back into my own middle and high school years, the "Computer Class" elective I took involved some coding in BASIC and playing games like "The Oregon Trail." While the BASIC instruction introduced a basic level of knowledge about how computers work and the logic underpinning their operation, it was a brief foray, and one I had to opt in to receive.

Current students need a broader, deeper, and more egalitarian exposure to technology. We live in the Information Age, and various electronic devices and services mediate large swaths of our daily lives. If we're to truly prepare students to be engaged citizens in a global society, we need to help them step back and recognize how technology is shaping their lives, experiences, and perceptions; and we need to help them understand some of the basic principles operating within the devices and services they interact with daily.

Technology mediates, and even drives, information behaviors. Technological literacy advances information literacy. Technology moderates how information is created, conveyed, and consumed; therefore, having an understanding of how information and media technologies function is fundamental to having a strong grasp of information literacy.

In short: We must find the time and make the room within instruction to teach technological literacy to our students.

TECHNOLOGICAL DISCERNMENT

Many students are handed technology at an early age and are allowed, and sometimes encouraged, to figure it out on their own. This leaves some holes in their understanding of what they're using and pushes much of the technology around them into the background of their consciousness.

On a very basic level, students need to be able to discern between a device, a service, and a platform. This may seem overly simplistic, but it is actually a fundamental piece of knowledge about living in a technologically oriented world.

Wi-Fi

While students might be able to identify that they need Wi-Fi for their device, they may not realize where Wi-Fi comes from. Ask a random sampling of students where the Wi-Fi router in their house is, and you'll be surprised by how few can answer. This is important for several reasons. First, they should know that Wi-Fi is not a free, open resource, but rather something paid for and monitored. Students should know another basic point about Wi-Fi: The closer a device is to a wireless router or access point, the stronger—and more stable—the internet connection. The fact that students did not understand this was never made clearer than during the pandemic lockdown when students would routinely lose their connection to remote classes as they wandered their homes with their devices.

Devices

Similarly, there are some common types of devices that have some basic architectural differences impacting how those devices can be used. For example, Chromebooks are extremely popular, both in school and at home. They are fundamentally different from a laptop or desktop computer in that their operating system (OS) is a specialized version of the Chrome web browser. This limits their functionality—users can't install programs on Chromebooks. And a Chromebook's functionality is severely limited if it is not able to connect to a wireless network. Also, because Chromebooks rarely have ethernet ports, the stability of audio and video streaming relies on Wi-Fi.

Chromebooks tend to have very small amounts of onboard memory. This limits what they are able to store onboard. Since Chromebooks are usually connected wirelessly to a cloud storage system, this isn't usually an issue. But if students are downloading images, audio, or video to their devices, they can quickly max out the storage capacity.

One other architectural element of Chromebooks that is sometimes not appreciated is that they are difficult to physically modify. Desktops, and to a lesser extent laptops, can often be opened up and upgraded one component at a time. This can keep old computers functioning for quite a while. It's much more difficult, if not impossible, to modify the hardware of a Chromebook. And Chromebooks come with a limited lifetime. They only receive updates to their OS for a set number of years after manufacture, not purchase, which means that buying an unsold, older model of a Chromebook means trading away some lifetime for a lower price. When the update period passes, Chromebooks will continue to function for a while, but as online apps and services evolve, the Chromebook will eventually lose its ability to work with them.

Chromebooks are just one type of device, and the above pieces of information can be quickly conveyed to students and reasserted at regular intervals to remind them of some basic principles. But hopefully, this provides a bit of insight into why educators need to offer some direct instruction on devices, even though it might at first glance seem rather basic.

Services

It is the work of a moment to find images shared online that show Facebook users typing in Google Search queries.[1] This is a vivid example that underlines an important technological literacy element. No teacher wants their students featured in the above example. This means that we need to help them understand that different services provide different kinds of information and interaction.

How many students could explain that the ubiquitous term "app" is short for "application"? And how many could then explain that "application" is another name for "program"? And, to carry it one step further, how many could explain the difference between using the online version of a service and using an app for the same service?

One particularly important area often ignored when discussing technology with students is one that has legal ramifications: terms of service. "It has become something of a common trope to note that online terms of service agreements are lengthy, obtuse, and universally ignored by the millions of users who bind themselves under these contracts every minute of every day" (Karanicolas 2021). Yet these terms of service set specific legal limits and liabilities by which users are generally bound. Such legal limitations are an important reason students should be inculcated with the habit of taking a moment to read the pop-ups that appear before clicking.

In addition to learning about their rights and responsibilities delineated in terms of service, it might also behoove students to learn about the exceptions to those terms. There are many examples of platforms that allow certain users more leeway when enforcing rules. This can be an important lesson not only in technology but also in civics.

CONSUMPTION, CURATION, AND CREATION

When considering how students interact with technology, it is valuable to consider the main modes of interaction available.

Consumption

The lowest level of technological interaction is consumption. In this mode, technology users take in content that has been created by others. This is generally a passive form of interaction. With auto-play features, there can be little or no need for input from the user once the consumption has been initiated.

In and of itself, nothing is wrong with consumption. But educators should regularly remind students that, as with food, consumption can be taken to excess, and that excess can be harmful to one's health—both physically and mentally. In 2019, more than 500 hours of video were uploaded to YouTube every minute.[2] It is literally impossible for a person to ingest all of the content available through that one website, never mind across the entirety of the internet. Therefore, we must help students learn how to deal with the onslaught of information. Helping them learn to curate the content they consume is a good first step.

Curation

Increasing one's technological interactions from consumption leads to curation. At this stage, users are engaging with content. They are making active selections about the types of content they want to consume and from which sources.

Curation is an incredibly important skill to build for our students. They are deluged with information. It is imperative that educators help students learn how to curate their information ecosystem. As with a physical ecosystem, one's information ecosystem can easily become polluted. But unlike with the physical environment, individuals have a much greater ability to avoid that pollution.

This is an area that overlaps with information literacy. It is difficult to overstate the importance of teaching students the basic principles of identifying whether information is reliable.

Creation

The most engaged technological interaction happens with creation. Here, users are actively utilizing technology to express their own ideas.

This is another area that overlaps with information literacy and digital citizenship. Students must recognize that while they can and should be creators, they must also give credit where it is due and be careful of how they utilize the work of others, either as inspiration or as an element in or basis of their own work. In addition to the legal ramifications of using work that is not their own, there are also important ethical considerations. This is an area ripe for discussion with students.

NAVIGATING TECHNOLOGY EFFECTIVELY, EFFICIENTLY, AND SAFELY

Keyboarding

While teachers give explicit instruction to young students in handwriting, it's still unfortunately rare for students to get typing instruction. While they may be wizards with their thumbs as they text and post from their phones, there are still a lot of academic activities that rely on using a standard keyboard. Watching students hunt and peck their way through assignments is painful, particularly when one considers how much time could be saved if students had typing instruction. This is a prime example of a skill that clearly is not "native" to students!

Typing may be the only skill I have used daily since it was drummed into me during a semester-long class in high school. I was motivated by watching my mother while visiting her at work; she could type 100 words a minute without breaking a sweat, a skill I envied when it was time to write my college applications.

School librarians are uniquely positioned to offer students important support in skills that might otherwise slip between the cracks of core classes. It would be very easy for a librarian to post links to free online typing tutor programs. This could be paired with typing challenges, contests, and even leaderboards. Students enjoy competing, and gamifying skill acquisition is a great way to motivate increased engagement.

Search Engines

"Genericization" occurs when a product name becomes so ubiquitous that the general public uses it to refer to any brand of that product. Some common examples might include asking for a Kleenex rather than a tissue, or a Band-Aid rather than an adhesive bandage, or Jell-O instead of gelatin.

Google has taken legal steps to push back on genericization, but it is rare to speak of online searching without hearing someone say they will "Google it." While this is in some ways humorous, it also points to several problems with how students, in particular, understand the technological tools they are employing.

First, the fact that "to Google" has become such a common usage as to have an entry in the Oxford English Dictionary masks a very fundamental problem: searchers may not realize that they are (or are not) using the actual Google search engine. Users of Apple products may "Google" information but are searching using Safari. There is also the fact that when "to Google" is used synonymously with online searching, users might not even realize that there are other search engine options available. Additionally, if "to Google" is synonymous for users with "research," fundamental communication issues might obscure what, precisely, searchers are actually doing when "researching." It is easily conceivable that a student says they "researched" the topic, which information professionals and educators might rightly think means the student used databases and scholarly resources to learn about a topic, when in reality, the student means, "I did a cursory open web search."

Next comes the issue of understanding how search engines provide results. Generally, search engines point to the most popular results. As anyone who's been a teenager knows, "popular" does not always mean "the best." Additionally, students may not realize that when they search for information online, the answer generally does not come from Google; rather, Google is simply pointing to websites that have information. This is particularly important when students receive "instant answer" results that are framed to look like *the* answer to a query. (See figure 8.1.)

While Google has gotten better at making sure to include citations and links for these types of answers, they can still be visually difficult for students to grasp if they do not know that they need to look. (When discussing online search, I regularly tell students that if someone asks where they got their information, the answer is *never* "Google."[3])

Steve Tetreault

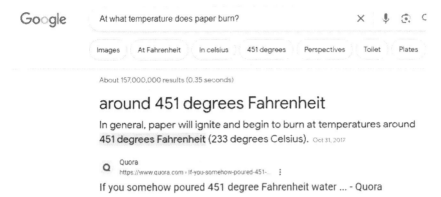

Figure 8.1 A Google Search for "At What Temperature Does Paper Burn?" Provides an Answer That Students Might Assume Comes Directly from Google if They Are Not Made Aware of the Fact that the Text beneath the Answer Indicates the Source of That Answer, Which in This Case Is Quora—a Site Composed of Community-Generated Answers to User-Posted Questions Which Should Not Be Considered a Definitive Source for Information. *Source*: Google Search Result: "At What Temperature Does Paper Burn?"

It is also important to discuss with students the "search bubble" phenomenon. Many are unaware that two different people doing the same Google search might get different sets of results, thanks to Google's use of personal information and past search history to tailor search results. Students need to be aware of the problematic facts involved when search engines try to provide "personalized" results. To anthropomorphize an algorithm, the search engine is making decisions about what it believes the searcher wants to see. That means it is omitting results that could be important for the searcher, either because they are looking for something outside their usual parameters, or because they might be inspired by unexpected results to take their search in a different direction.

As a side note to online search histories, it would behoove students to know that using "incognito" mode does not hide their search history from the service they are using.

One additional area for potential instruction is teaching students about custom search engines (CSEs). Google offers a free, easy-to-use CSE tool that allows users to build a search engine that only draws answers from a set list of sources. In other words, it's possible to create search engines that only pull information from curated, reliable resources and/or are focused on a particular topic. This can be fun for students, but it can also help them learn how to build their own search tools that will provide them with more reliable results than an open web search, without the costs often associated with databases.

In addition to discussing the mechanics of search engines, students need instruction in search strategies. This is a topic covered by information literacy instruction.

ALGORITHMS

Students need to have at least a basic understanding of the existence of algorithms as an architectural element of online search engines and various content delivery systems. While many may have heard the term thrown around, particularly over the past few years, they may not understand what the term means in a practical sense.

Recently, it was found that YouTube's video recommendation algorithm was driving those with right-wing political tendencies toward increasingly radicalized content.[4] YouTube has since implemented measures meant to mitigate this unfortunate aspect of their video recommendation system. However, the underlying principle is one that can be seen in many online services and platforms.

Many algorithms are tuned to reward intense emotional reactions.[5] This is an incredibly effective way of getting users to engage with platforms—users are "rewarded" with likes and upvotes and reactions, while also building up and reinforcing parasocial bonds. And it is an unfortunate tendency of the human mind that it tends to focus on the "negative" elements it encounters. So it is easy for online algorithms to create a spiral of increasingly negative content.[6]

As far back as 2009, a Pew Research Center survey found that 61 percent of American adults do an online search for medical information before they consult with a medical professional.[7] This demonstrates the quantity of users who seek medical information online. More recently, and more disturbingly, a research study conducted in partnership with Amnesty International found that TikTok's algorithm pushes teen users toward harmful mental health content.[8] This is troubling on multiple levels, as teenagers might be especially prone to manipulation on social media.[9] As search engines and social media sites often utilize algorithms to determine what content to serve users, students need an understanding of the foundations of algorithms to protect their physical, mental, and emotional health.

Additionally, research has found that misinformation travels faster online than truth.[10] This is in no small part due to algorithms. One particularly important and disturbing example of algorithms creating issues is the fact that algorithmic ad placement systems often funnel money to misinformation sources because those sources tend to be widely and quickly shared. This, in turn, spurs misinformation sources to produce more content in a vicious cycle that rewards escalating fabricated content. Also, social media algorithms are frequently set up to promote information that is receiving high interaction.

Misinformation is more likely to receive interaction than factual information, due in large part to the strong emotional reaction misinformation often elicits.

Another important way algorithms affect our daily lives is through the construction of filter bubbles. As online services gather more information about individual users, those services' algorithms are set up to encourage greater use of and engagement with that service. To that end, a service's algorithms attempt to serve users content the algorithms believe the user will interact with, increasing the users' time on the service. This leads to the creation of a filter bubble, an online space that provides specific types of content to a user. In effect, a filter bubble preemptively removes content from a user's online experience, limiting their knowledge of and exposure to ideas or information the algorithm thinks are likely to decrease a user's use of the service. Students need to know that what they see online is often moderated by algorithms, which pick and choose what to show them without the users' knowledge.

DIGITAL CITIZENSHIP

One of the primary purposes of public education is to produce informed, capable, and engaged citizens. As our students are coming of age in a technologically oriented society, we must include digital citizenship as part of their curricula.

The barriers to entry for technology have steadily decreased over the past several decades. Costs have dropped, and ease of use has increased. It is possible for toddlers to operate devices with visually oriented tactile user interfaces. However, this does not mean that they are capable of using devices well or wisely. As children need models and instruction to learn how to become good citizens within their community, they need the same scaffolding to learn how to become good digital citizens.

Citation as Digital Citizenship

One element of good digital citizenship that is easy to overlook is encouraging students to always cite sources. This is an important concept for several reasons. First, we should always encourage students to give credit where it is due. While social media has made resharing posts incredibly easy, it has not done a good job of indicating the original source of reshared posts. In an age where copying and pasting is the work of a few key clicks, it's important to instill in students a respect for the work of others. This should include citing sources.

Citing sources goes back to reliability—we want our students to be sources of reliable information online. This means they need to provide sourcing for what they share online, particularly when the individual student is not the source of ideas, images, audio, video, or information that they share. Doing so enhances the information environment and reduces misinformation.

Additionally, by encouraging students to cite sources, we instill in them an expectation that others will cite sources as well. When citation is an automatic part of their information sharing, it becomes an expected part of their information landscape. Thus, if they encounter unsourced information online, they will be more skeptical of accepting it at face value. This improves not only their own online experiences but also the larger information environment. Students who expect citation in online information sharing become stewards of this particular element of good digital citizenship.

Online Safety

As too many librarians have learned, it is easy to rile up a base of people within an echo chamber by making false claims. Research has shown that anonymity might be a factor in increasing aggressiveness online, but a larger factor is the modeling of aggressive behavior as a norm within an online environment.[11] Therefore, it's important for educators to model non-aggressive online behavior, particularly in a computer-mediated context. As educators, we need to make sure our students understand that there are people on the other end of their comments.

We also need to encourage students to advocate for their own safety online. One of the most insidious things about social media is that, unless you are the one under attack, only you and your attackers are likely to know the assault you're facing. Again, this is something too many librarians have personal experience with. While there is widespread knowledge of the ongoing censorship pushes and book bans within the library community, the public at large has been extremely slow in learning about these situations.

Educators have the obligation to help students be safe, engaged, and productive members of a democratic society. This includes helping them learn how to be good digital citizens and how to deal with others online who don't exhibit good digital citizenship or those who seek to inflict emotional, mental, or physical harm on them. This includes helping students learn how to take screenshots of harmful messages they receive and learn to whom they should report such messaging.

This is an area with both physical and online components. As previously mentioned, students should be more aware of the terms of service they agree to, including what constitutes a violation of those terms, and to whom they can report violations. Educators should also familiarize students with the school and local law enforcement personnel who can provide support if they receive harmful online messaging.

It is also imperative that we regularly remind students to consider what information they post online. We are all familiar with the safety issues involved in sharing personal details, particularly contact and location information. But the recent increase in the availability of artificial intelligence (AI) has added some new dimensions to consider. A recent commercial targeted at parents highlighted the potential dangers of posting images of one's child online; in it, the commercial's producer took from online a picture of a child and used AI to create a video replica that illustrated how an image can be manipulated to say and do anything.[12] While this type of technology has existed for a while, the very prominent case of Taylor Swift being used as the subject of a series of AI-generated pornographic images makes this danger more clear.[13,14]

Another element of technological literacy related to safety is the importance of password security. We often consider password security to be an online issue; however, with the spread of the "Internet of Things"—internet-connected devices throughout a home—password security is now also an analog world security issue. Students should also understand that sharing passwords with family is okay, but sharing a network password with someone they don't know well can open their home to a variety of risks. Additionally, when students are out in the world, they should recognize that open Wi-Fi networks can be a security hazard of which they should be wary.

FINDING AND EVALUATING SOURCES OF INFORMATION

While research and source evaluation are information literacy issues, they are also technology issues. A 2022 survey found that 78 percent of teenage respondents reported going to social media as their primary method of seeking information.[15] Another survey found that when it comes to seeking medical information, younger information consumers are increasingly likely to seek answers online before consulting a medical professional; and, research from the University of Arizona College of Medicine found that "Four in 10 posts about liver disease on TikTok contain misinformation."[16] This is just the tip of the medical misinformation iceberg, and medical care is not the only area where misinformation is rampant.

It's important, therefore, to clarify with students the differences inherent in various information technologies. For much of the internet's history, educators have encouraged careful consideration of print sources ahead of online sources, for a variety of reasons. Those reasons are no less valid now than they were in the early days of the internet's introduction to classrooms.

It is unlikely that students will turn en masse to print resources, but it's worth pointing out to them that print sources are not malleable like online sources—what is printed stays as it is, while it's often quite easy to make changes to online sources. Print can also make for a good point of analogy to help students understand architectural elements of the online world.

As an example: Websites are like books—they contain collections of (web) pages that are often subdivided and categorized by topic. Unlike print sources, websites are extremely inexpensive, or even free, to create and publish. This lowers the threshold of who can distribute information. There are pros and cons to the democratization of publication ability—ones students should consider and discuss. Of particular note should be the fact that there are few limits on what can be posted or how online sites present themselves. While it's not impossible to do the same with printed materials, there tend to be many more checks in place to guard against misinformation and misrepresentation in traditional print media because of the financial costs involved in producing those materials.

EVALUATING DEVICES AND SERVICES

In addition to understanding some of the architectural structures of the technologies they use, students must be introduced to some of the economic realities on which much of their digital world is built. Too many people live by a part of writer and thinker Stewart Brand's quote, "Information wants to be free." There is a widely held belief that one shouldn't have to pay for information, nor for the apps that provide access to it. As educators who are often faced with limited budgets, "free" is a favorite word.

It's important to recognize the full message of Brand's quote, however:

[I]nformation sort of wants to be expensive because it is so valuable—the right information in the right place just changes your life. On the other hand, information almost wants to be free because the costs of getting it out is getting lower and lower all of the time. So you have these two things fighting against each other.[17]

This quote gets closer to the truth of the digitization of information. The cost of accessing information is, indeed, getting lower and lower. And there is also a recognition that there is value in information. However, this quote misses several important points.

Information wants to be expensive because high-quality information is expensive to produce. High-quality information requires collection by a trained observer and review and certification by fact-checkers. Few people in the world are willing or able to invest the time and energy needed to train in, produce, and disseminate high-quality information for free. We need to acknowledge this reality and encourage students to understand that paying for information can be one of the indicators of a high-quality source.

As important, if not more so, is familiarizing students with the saying, "If you're not paying for it, you're the product." Many apps and online resources generate revenue by gathering and selling information about their users. While there may be a vague notion that this is happening, it is likely that the vast majority of users are unaware that information about their every move within each online interaction is harvested. And now "smart" devices are also harvesting additional data, utilizing built-in cameras and microphones to gather data about users from the users' physical environment. The privacy

Steve Tetreault

implications of this economic model of "free" technology should be a cornerstone of technological literacy instruction.

ARTIFICIAL INTELLIGENCE AND TECHNOLOGICAL LITERACY

While forms of AI have existed for a long time, the recent boom in "generative" AI has caught many educators—and many members of the public—off guard. Whereas anyone currently in education grew up in a world in which technology might have mediated the creation or dissemination of information, our students are now growing up in a world where machines can "create" information. It's imperative that we help them understand how this happens and help them start considering what it means for the information environment in which they live.

Part of the problem here is that little publicly shared information details the precise methods through which companies are creating and "training" their AI tools. However, we do know that the field is rapidly evolving, requiring careful consideration and monitoring to understand the latest additions to and applications of AI.

There are ethical and legal considerations that should be part of any conversation about AI in education. Currently, companies "train" AI by feeding it massive amounts of data and having the AI learn how to find connections among and across those data. In order to capture those massive collections of data, companies are utilizing both public domain resources as well as copyrighted, trademarked, and private data they are able to "scrape" from online sources such as social media accounts. I would suggest there is no age group too young to discuss whether one should be allowed to use someone else's work without their permission to create something based on that work.

There are also the ethical, legal, and economic considerations of how AI is already impacting a variety of professions. Indeed, the 2023 Writers Guild of America strike and the 2023 Screen Actors Guild strike famously included a hard-fought battle over whether studios should have the right to use AI to write scripts or produce AI versions of actors that can be employed in place of the actors themselves.[18] Media outlets have also increasingly used AI to generate various types of information.

We also know that this technology has a physical impact on the environment. AI engines require massive amounts of electricity, as well as massive amounts of water to keep the machines on which they're running at operating temperatures. Worsening the problem is the fact that studies have found the environmental impacts of AI are generally borne by those of lower socioeconomic status.[19]

By the same token, there are some who feel AI might help discover ways to alleviate the effects it is having on the world.[20] It is undeniable that some very useful elements of AI exist within education. For educators, AI can offer many ways to increase productivity and expedite materials preparation. As an example, an educator can feed a text into an AI engine and request that the AI convert the Lexile level to meet the needs of particular students. Educators can also use AI to almost instantly generate lesson plans, study guides, assessments, visuals, presentations, and more.

We know students are likely to use AI, either covertly or overtly, to help them complete some assignments. This requires educators to think about how they can alter their instruction to either mitigate the usefulness of AI to the assignment or incorporate uses for AI within the assignment. Either way, educators need to make students aware of the fact that AI is still a developing technology. When asked to draw on research and cite sources, there is currently a high likelihood that AI will fabricate information. To the user who does not already have a thorough education within the topic at hand, these "hallucinated" instances are likely to pass unnoticed. Thus, helping students learn about and with AI seems much more likely to have positive outcomes for students than simply attempting to ban the use of AI in education.

CONCLUSION

Technological Literacy: A Return to Luddism

For years, the term "Luddite" has referred to a person who is opposed to any type of technology. "Luddite" was used disparagingly, as a shorthand term for someone stuck in an antiquated past and refusing to engage with the reality of the present or prepare for the future. Recently, the term has enjoyed a bit of a revival and a return to its roots.

The term arose during the early 1800s, during England's Industrial Revolution. The full story is fascinating and well worth learning about. But the reason the term is making something of a comeback is because the original Luddites were not anti-technology. Rather, they were pro-humanity. As factory owners started using technology to replace—and in some cases, endanger—workers, the workers called for a path that would allow them to continue making a living wage while finding ways to utilize the benefits provided by technology.

The workers were unsuccessful in their attempts to place safety and humanity ahead of profit, and the victors are the ones who write the histories. Eventually, the name of their movement became synonymous with being stuck in the past and afraid of the future.

As educators, we owe it to our students to carry forward the original mission of the Luddites: to put the humanity and safety of our students ahead of a focus on the "next big thing" and a worship of efficiency. Technological literacy is a way to do this, to help students understand that technology cannot replace kindness, that efficiency should not replace empathy, and that speed should not replace thoughtfulness.

Steve Tetreault

Technological Literacy Is Just Good Education

Students are human, and humans are analog creatures who live in an analog world that is increasingly mediated by digital technologies. Humans cannot be "digital natives"; we can only learn to use digital tools to supplement our analog abilities to understand the world around us. As educators, it is incumbent that we recognize this reality and take steps to help familiarize our students with the architecture and ideas upon which the digital infrastructure is built. While students may utilize digital resources for long periods of time, that does not make them experts in understanding technology. And educators should not shy away from encouraging students to share their uses and understandings of technology as part of lessons. Educators can learn from students. However, we cannot cede authority over learning about technology to students. They are children, and as clever as children can be, they are not experienced or learned. That's why we require them to attend school for most of their adolescence— so they can learn how to learn, how to examine the world around them, and how to be critical thinkers and critical consumers of information.

Technological literacy must become one of the core disciplines for students. This does not require educators to be intimately familiar with the details of every latest and greatest piece of technology. What it requires is a recognition of the foundations on which technologies, whether services or devices, are built, and a willingness to examine and consider how current and future iterations of technology build on those foundations. This does not require educators to be the "sage on the stage" in lessons on technological literacy. In fact, students would be better served if educators let students share their knowledge in the area, giving them agency and voice, and then serving as a "guide on the side" to help students add to their knowledge.

Obviously, this wisdom is not limited to technological literacy; it's best practice for any subject. Although we may think of the digital world as a new area or a space of the future, learning is as old as humanity. We should bear that in mind as we embrace technological literacy, and as we help students see that no matter how new something is, it was built on a base of knowledge and experience.

ADDITIONAL RESOURCES

- "Applied Digital Skills" (Google). https://applieddigitalskills.withgoogle .com/s/en/home.
- "Be Internet Awesome" (Google). https://beinternetawesome.withgoogle .com/en_us/.
- "CS First" (Google). https://csfirst.withgoogle.com/s/en/home.
- "Let's Get (Info) Lit! Lessons, Resources, & Ideas for Teaching Information Literacy" (Steve Tetreault). bit.ly/getinfolit.

NOTES

1. "There's a Facebook Page Called 'Google Search Engine,' and It Has Some People Very Confused," *Reddit*. https://www.reddit.com/r/oldpeoplefacebook/comments/22bin1/theres_a_facebook_page_called_google_search/?rdt=62788.
2. Susan Wojcicki, "YouTube at 15: My Personal Journey and the Road Ahead," *YouTube Official Blog*, February 14, 2020. https://blog.youtube/news-and-events/youtube-at-15-my-personal-journey/.
3. Tetreault, "Argument and Debate Lesson 17: Online Terms and Trustworthiness."
4. Alex Russell, "YouTube Video Recommendations Lead to More Extremist Content for Right-Leaning Users, Researchers Suggest," UC Davis. https://www.ucdavis.edu/curiosity/news/youtube-video-recommendations-lead-more-extremist-content-right-leaning-users-researchers.
5. Filippo Menczer, "Facebook Whistleblower Frances Haugen Testified That the Company's Algorithms Are Dangerous — Here's How They Can Manipulate You," *The Conversation*, October 7, 2021. https://theconversation.com/facebook-whistleblower-frances-haugen-testified-that-the-companys-algorithms-are-dangerous-heres-how-they-can-manipulate-you-169420.
6. Brady and The Conversation US, "Social Media Algorithms Warp How People Learn from Each Other," *Scientific American*, August 25, 2023. https://www.scientificamerican.com/article/social-media-algorithms-warp-how-people-learn-from-each-other/.
7. Pew Research Center, "61% of American Adults Look Online for Health Information." https://www.pewresearch.org/internet/2009/06/11/61-of-american-adults-look-online-for-health-information/.
8. Amnesty International, "Global: TikTok's 'For You' Feed Risks Pushing Children and Young People towards Harmful Mental Health Content." https://amnesty.org/en/latest/news/2023/11/tiktok-risks-pushing-children-towards-harmful-content/.
9. The Annie E. Casey Foundation, "Social Media's Concerning Effect on Teen Mental Health," *The Annie E. Casey Foundation Blog*, August 10, 2023. https://www.aecf.org/blog/generation-z-and-mental-health.
10. Peter Dizikes, "Study: On Twitter, False News Travels Faster than True Stories," *MIT News*, March 8, 2018. https://news.mit.edu/2018/study-twitter-false-news-travels-faster-true-stories-0308.
11. Leonie Rösner and Nicole Krämer, "Verbal Venting in the Social Web: Effects of Anonymity and Group Norms on Aggressive Language Use in Online Comments," *Social Media + Society* 2 (August 16, 2016).
12. Deutsche Telekom, "Don't Share Your Kids Personal Information—without Consent—Deutsche Telekom Deepfake AI Ad." https://www.topview.ai/blog/detail/Don-t-share-your-kids-personal-information-Without-Consent-Deutsche-Telekom-Deepfake-AI-Ad.
13. Samantha Murphy Kelly, "It's Not Just Taylor Swift: AI-Generated Porn Is Targeting Women and Kids All over the World," *CNN Business*, January 26, 2024. https://omaha.com/news/nation-world/article_a5981034-d98c-5b7a-b0f7-678843023c73.html.
14. Note: This situation also highlights the problematic state of affairs surrounding culpability for the distribution of such material; in this particular instance, the images

were reportedly available on the social media site X for at least seventeen hours before they were removed, and that was only because of a massive backlash from Swift's fans. Other AI-generated pornography that utilizes the likenesses of real people has continued to stay up on sites despite multiple reports to the hosting sites. Unfortunately, many victims do not have the social clout of mega-star Swift to help direct attention to their situation.

15. McGraw Hill, "Student Study Habits Have Changed. McGraw Hill Responds with the SHARPEN™ Study App," *PR Newswire*, October 4, 2022. https://www.prnewswire.com/news-releases/student-study-habits-have-changed-mcgraw-hill-responds-with-the-sharpen-study-app-301639772.html.

16. Digestive Disease Week, "TikTok Hosts the Latest Dance Moves and Bad Information on Liver Disease." https://medicalxpress.com/news/2023-05-tiktok-hosts-latest-bad-liver.html#:~:text=TikTok%20hosts%20the%20latest%20dance%20moves%20and%20bad%20information%20on%20liver%20disease,-by%20Digestive%20Disease&text=Four%20in%2010%20posts%20about,Disease%20Week%20(DDW)%202023.

17. Joshua Gans, "'Information Wants to Be Free': The History of That Quote," Digitalopoly | Competition in the Digital Age. https://digitopoly.org/2015/10/25/information-wants-to-be-free-the-history-of-that-quote/#:~:text=On%20the%20one%20hand%20information,two%20fighting%20against%20each%20other.

18. Angela Watercutter, "The Hollywood Strikes Stopped AI from Taking Your Job. But for How Long?" *Wired*, December 25, 2023. https://www.wired.com/story/hollywood-saved-your-job-from-ai-2023-will-it-last/.

19. David Danelski, "AI Creates New Environmental Injustices, But There's a Fix," *University of California, Riverside | News*, July 12, 2023. https://news.ucr.edu/articles/2023/07/12/ai-creates-new-environmental-injustices-theres-fix.

20. Jude Coleman, "AI's Climate Impact Goes beyond Its Emissions," *Scientific American*, December 7, 2023. https://www.scientificamerican.com/article/ais-climate-impact-goes-beyond-its-emissions/.

9

Preparing School Librarians to Integrate Visual Literacy Using Artificial Intelligence

Lesley S. J. Farmer, Professor of Library Media, California State University Long Beach, California

School librarians are needed more than ever to deal with artificial intelligence (AI), particularly new generative AI tools that can produce realistic text and images. People often trust images more than text, assuming that images are less likely to be manipulated. The result? Those same people may make bad decisions and act on them, causing negative consequences, such as idealized body images that drive girls to unhealthy diets. At the same time, these tools—and educators' heightened interest in them—can be leveraged to increase visual literacy instruction and practice.

Because AI is such a hot topic, it can serve as a gateway to gaining visual literacy more generally. Moreover, as information professionals, school librarians provide physical and intellectual access to visual sources across subject matters, so they are well-positioned to foster visual literacy.

Thus, this chapter discusses visual literacy using an AI lens and suggests ways to prepare school librarians so they can help their school communities gain expertise in these arenas.

LITERACIES

AI itself, although it has been around since World War II, became more popular in the 1980s with the concept of expert systems. In comparison, generative AI has come into its own only in the 2020s, thanks to the big data and large language models alongside machine learning advances. In terms of literacy, AI may be considered a subset of digital literacy: the ability to effectively and responsibly locate, comprehend, evaluate, use, and create using technology. Recently, some educators have deemed AI literacy a specific set of skills that focuses on generative AI: knowing how AI works; detecting AI-generated sources; using prompt engineering (i.e., how to pose good questions); using representative AI image generator tools; determining what AI image generators do better, the same, or worse than other tools or humans; using AI image generators to support creativity and originating knowledge; and knowing about AI image generator policies. To that end, educators, including librarians, should know how AI image generators can be incorporated into education and the workplace (i.e., to support productivity and gain knowledge).[1]

Visual literacy predates even written literacy, yet it is probably more relevant than ever. Even prehistoric humans needed visual literacy to cope with their environment, such as interpreting visual weather "signs." Visual literacy is a learned set of skills and knowledge, not an innate ability, and is a complex process. The eye normally sees the entire visual image at once, with 30 percent of the brain's cortex devoted to visual processing, in contrast to 3 percent of the cortex devoted to hearing. Furthermore, some visual principles are socially and culturally defined, such as connotations of color (e.g., death associated with black or white).

As with information and digital literacy, visual literacy includes the effective and responsible ability to locate, comprehend, evaluate, use, and create visual "messages." Nowadays, visual literacy encompasses all media (still including nature). In any case, the Association of College and Research Libraries (ACRL)'s 2022 visual literacy framework defines visual literacy as follows:

> Visual literacy is a set of abilities that enables an individual to effectively find, interpret, evaluate, use, and create images and visual media. Visual literacy skills equip a learner to understand and analyze the contextual, cultural, ethical, aesthetic, intellectual, and technical components involved in the production and use of visual materials. A visually literate individual is both a critical consumer of visual media and a competent contributor to a body of shared knowledge and culture. (p. 1)[2]

Since that definition was developed, ACRL has recognized the expanded visual information landscape, its increasing role in communication while more critical discernment is needed, the impact of culture on its development and use, and the need for social justice through visually literate usage.

VISUAL LITERACY ASPECTS IN AI

Addressing AI through a visual literacy lens offers an effective way to gain expertise in both arenas. AI draws upon existing images to generate images, which might be misleading, and it can facilitate data visualizations, which also

Lesley S. J. Farmer

might be misleading. Therefore, visual literacy is important for viewers so they can dive beyond the surface to determine reality and deduce the intended meaning.

Avgerinou and Pettersson[3] framed visual literacy as a set of domains with visual perception as the core process: visual language, visual learning, visual thinking, and visual communication:

- Visual language consists of the elements of art (line, shape, color, form, space, and texture) and the principles of design (balance, harmony, rhythm, movement, proportion, emphasis, variety, and unity), which compose the elements into an image. These elements operate the same way in AI.
- Visual learning encompasses the ability to decode, analyze, and interpret images and their messages, as well as appreciate their aesthetic value. Although not mentioned in this framework, the context of the image (i.e., source, social-cultural, situational) impacts the interpretation. The researchers also posited that visual literacy improves learning. With AI-generated images, the viewer also needs to know how AI generates those images, using algorithms to synthesize image specifications by drawing upon and manipulating available data sets. Further complicating this aspect, most AI image generators do not identify or cite their own sources.
- Visual thinking implies that one can use visuals as information sources and tools to address issues and solve problems. In the context of AI, prompt engineering (i.e., designing queries or instructions to elicit desired AI responses) exemplifies this domain.
- Visual communication consists of effectively using visual language to represent ideas that are then shared with others. This domain constitutes the creative, generative side of visual literacy. In AI parlance, visual communication again uses prompt engineering, but for external purposes rather than internal processing/thinking.

Some specific visual literacy techniques facilitate the discernment of AI-generated images, which can then help viewers assess the validity of those images and aid in interpreting the creators' intentions. With that visual knowledge, viewers can decide how to value and respond to those images. A sampling of strategies follows:

- Check for inconsistencies, such as ten columns merging into nine (often evidenced by blurred lines).
- Look for details that don't make sense, such as sharks in swimming pools.
- Check for details that are too consistent, such as hair texture.
- Does the image, such as a face, look too symmetrical?

- Does the image seem somehow "hyper-realistic" or too "plastic" to be real? This reaction is called the "uncanny valley," and it makes people feel uncomfortable. Examples are robots that seem too human or movies with Computer-Generated Imagery-created humans.
- Examine fine details (e.g., eyes, hands, teeth, texture). Humans have very sharp visual acuity when observing faces; it is a survival tool.[4]
- Know your science principles (e.g., optics, gravity), such as differences in lighting from one area of an image to another.[5]
- Consider the source. Is the media outlet or website reputable?
- Analyze the image's metadata if available.
- Check the context of the image; what is the accompanying text, if any? Is it propaganda or misinformation?
- Do a reverse image search.[6]
- Use AI detection tools.[7]
- Use fact-checking tools.[8]

As noted above, visual literacy also entails the ability to use visual elements and principles to create aesthetic and meaningful images. There are several ways to leverage visual literacy to generate AI images, either as the product or as a starting point to inspire original image creation.

- Leverage visual design principles, such as placing the key detail in the center or having lines point to it (e.g., a race's winner).
- Employ color theory to convey mood, such as light colors to convey joy or youthfulness.
- Leverage typography to underscore meaning, such as Gothic letters for text about the Middle Ages.
- Be culturally sensitive to the use of color (e.g., Vietnamese brides often wear red instead of white).
- Take advantage of symbols, such as country flags, stop signs, or stars.
- Consider your audience. Will they understand the connotation, such as a dial phone, or misinterpret a symbol (e.g., owls in some cultures connote wisdom, but in other cultures connote evil)?

VISUAL LITERACY AND GENERATIVE AI EDUCATION

Sadly, visual literacy education is largely undervalued and unevenly implemented. Furthermore, over the years, visual arts education has also decreased in frequency in formal education.[9] To discern the news literacy of middle and high school students, for instance, Farmer[10] surveyed the students' librarians, who stated that students' weakest news literacy skill was discerning faked images—and the curriculum didn't address that skill. Similarly, in assessing postsecondary students' visual literacy performance, Brumberger[11] found that

Lesley S. J. Farmer

they were not adept at interpreting or producing visuals and had little visual literacy instruction. Stanford's national survey of students from middle school to college level found that students were not news-literate, including visual literacy aspects, and urged relevant curricula to address this issue.[12]

The need for visual literacy education is apparent, and AI-generated images elevate that need even more. Certainly, for school librarians, AI image generators such as DALL-E raise issues of bias and misinformation. The products generated are only as good as the source pool that they draw from, and the algorithms themselves are originally constructed by humans, which then adds another dimension of bias. Furthermore, the use of such source material also highlights legal and ethical issues of intellectual property rights. Even sharing the process by which AI can generate information can enlighten the library's clientele and motivate them to develop and use critical thinking skills more often.

Discussing the impact of AI image generators also constitutes a valuable visual literacy lesson. Drawing upon existing materials, AI seems to seamlessly synthesize digital information, which can jump-start information tasks such as research, coding, and visual arts creation. Such AI tools are already impacting how artists and programmers work. At the same time, librarians should point out that the original sources of information are seldom identified, which brings up the importance of attribution and intellectual property.

More specifically, current AI tools can generate a huge variety of believable images, which thus entail visual literacy skills: using the "language" of imagery to comprehend, analyze, interpret, and communicate with images appropriately and critically. These skills are obviously applied to all types of visual images: 2- and 3-D art, film, and television, as well as digital images.

PREPARING SCHOOL LIBRARIANS TO INTEGRATE VISUAL LITERACY THROUGH AI

If visual literacy in AI is such an obvious area for learning, then why is it not in the curriculum? One reason may stem from the fact that many educators, including school librarians, do not have a strong background in visual literacy.[13] Fortunately, librarians know how to find high-quality information, including visual expert inputs, about visual literacy. Furthermore, librarians know how to collaborate so that they can complement one another's knowledge bases. For instance, the more that viewers understand physics principles such as optics, the less likely they will be fooled by AI-generated images or other manipulated images.

Because it cannot be assumed that preservice school librarians have experienced formal visual literacy education, let alone AI instruction, librarian educators should ensure that such training is incorporated into their curricula. Visual literacy and AI can intertwine to be incorporated into several aspects of school librarianship and associated courses: productivity (e.g., designing flyers and posters), programming (e.g., AI imaging tool workshops, visiting artists who use AI), collection development (e.g., selecting AI imaging apps, creating bibliographies about visual AI), and instruction (e.g., linking search queries and prompt engineering, determining the source and validity of images, interpreting AI images, addressing the legal and ethical aspects of AI imaging). In each case, preservice school librarians learn how to be effective AI image consumers, then producers and teachers.

Here is a sampling of learning activities that can engage preservice (and in-service) school librarians in gaining visual literacy skills using a generative AI context. In most cases, librarian educators should foster constructivist active learning. They should also ask their preservice school librarian students to reflect on their learning experiences and consider strategies to teach the school community these skills.

- Research how algorithms and generative AI image generators are developed.
- Track the evolution of AI imaging.
- Investigate ways that AI-generated images impact students specifically and society more generally.
- Identify visual elements and principles employed in AI-generated images.
- Analyze and critique AI-generated images.
- Investigate how AI-generated images represent gender, ethnicity, and other social identifiers.
- Trace AI-generated image sources and their citations (which are often bogus or use copyrighted images without attribution or permission).
- Compare image source-tracking tools to see how successful they are.
- Test the same AI prompt to see if different images emerge when done at a different time or using a different AI image generator.
- Explore ways that AI-generated images can support the conceptualization of ideas such as mind mapping and data representations.
- Show how transforming information from one format to another (e.g., text to image) impacts the information, exemplifying transliteracy.
- Research legal and ethical concerns about DALL-E and other AI image generators.
- Locate, critique, and improve policies about AI image generators and their use.
- Analyze case studies where AI image generator use led to plagiarism.
- Interview artists and programmers to discuss their use of AI image generators.

As part of experiential learning, preservice school librarians can collaborate with classroom teachers to identify ways to address visual AI use

Lesley S. J. Farmer

in class. This effort can serve as a catalyst for addressing visual literacy more generally. Such activities can be done as a professional development event or implemented with K–12 students as coursework, a library program, or a co-curricular activity. Efforts may also result in a schoolwide set of guidelines or policies about AI, as well as visual literacy in the curriculum. The following learning activity ideas can front-load librarian and teacher brainstorming:

- Use AI-generated images to jump-start students' writing or artwork.
- Have students prompt engineers image in class to build their query/search techniques.
- Have students transform AI content into another format (e.g., text to image, or image to text).
- Use AI image generators as a tool to provide a visualization of a subject area (e.g., locale, historical event, science processes, gender roles, or stereotypes), which can then be critiqued in terms of accuracy.
- Have students analyze news or advertising images to determine if they are AI-generated.

Brown et al.'s 2016 textbook *Visual Literacy for Libraries* offers visual literacy concepts for higher education, many of which can be adapted to K–12 settings.[14] For K–8 teachers, Moline's 2011 book *I See What You Mean*[15] provides teachers with strategies to help K–8 students comprehend visual products such as diagrams, graphs, and maps. The following websites can also facilitate visual literacy learning:

- https://www.dawsoncollege.qc.ca/ai/portfolios/seeing-is-not-believing -visual-literacy-in-the-age-of-ai/
- https://www.nytimes.com/2021/03/17/learning/lesson-of-the-day-your -loved-ones-and-eerie-tom-cruise-videos-reanimate-unease-with-deep- fakes.html
- https://cphmag.com/thoughts-ai/
- https://mediumisthemessage.eu/ai-in-the-classroom-visual-literacy-cre- ativity-and-authorship/
- https://docs.google.com/document/d/1J6C4aIqWZjl8i1H-GmPxVKZ M7jpYgHJMfcPu6wHksXl/edit
- https://www.techlearning.com/news/best-free-ai-image-generators-for -teachers
- https://www.ala.org/acrl/sites/ala.org.acrl/files/content/standards/ Framework_Companion_Visual_Literacy.pdf

AI image generators offer a unique opportunity to rethink information literacy and align it with today's technology. Indeed, current school librarians have a once-in-a-lifetime opportunity to experience a new set of technology tools from the ground up. How exciting!

NOTES

1. Casal-Otero, Lorena, Alejandro Catala, Carmen Fernández-Morante, Maria Taboada, Beatriz Cebreiro, and Senén Barro, "AI Literacy in K-12: A Systematic Literature Review," *International Journal of STEM Education*, 10, no. 1 (2023). https://doi.org/10.1186/s40594-023-00418-7.
2. Association of College Research Libraries, "ACRL Visual Literacy Competency Standards for Higher Education," 2011. https://www.ala.org/acrl/standards/visualliteracy.
3. Avgerinou, Maria, and Rune Pettersson, "Toward a Cohesive Theory of Visual Literacy," *Journal of Visual Literacy*, 30, no. 2 (2011): 1–19.
4. Steele, Chandra, "Can You Spot AI-Generated Images? Take Our Quiz to Test Your Skills," *PC Mag*, March 7, 2024. https://www.pcmag.com/how-to/how-to-detect-ai-created-images.
5. Wen, Tiffanie, "The Hidden Signs that can Reveal a Fake Photo," *BBC*, June 9, 2020. https://www.bbc.com/future/article/20170629-the-hidden-signs-that-can-reveal-if-a-photo-is-fake.
6. McCoy, Julia, "11 Best Image Search Engines for Visual Content," *Search Engine Journal*, July 18, 2022. https://www.searchenginejournal.com/best-image-search-engines/299963/.
7. See: https://www.aiornot.com/.
8. Snelling, Jennifer, "Top 10 Sites to Help Students Check Their Facts," International Society of Technology in Education.
9. Anderson, Elizabeth, Maria Avgerinou, Stavi Dimas, and Rhonda Robinson, "Visual Literacy in the K12 Classroom of the 21st Century: From College Preparation to Finding One's Own Voice," In *Handbook of Research on K-12 Blended and Virtual Learning through the I²flex Classroom Model*, IGI Global, 2021. https://www.igi-global.com/chapter/visual-literacy-in-the-k12-classroom-of-the-21st-century/275561.
10. Lesley Farmer, "News Literacy and Fake News Curriculum: School Librarians' Perceptions of Pedagogical Practices," *Journal of Media Literacy Education*, 11, no. 3 (2019): 1–11.
11. Brumberger, Eva, "Visual Literacy and the Digital Native: An Examination of the Millennial Learner," *Journal of Visual Literacy*, 30, no. 1 (2011): 19–47. https://search.ebscohost.com/login.aspx?direct=true&db=eric&AN=EJ931652&site=ehost-live http://www.ohio.edu/visualliteracy/JVL_ISSUE_ARCHIVES/JVL30(1)/30_1_Brumberger.pdf.
12. Breakstone, Joel, Mark Smith, Sam Wineburg, Amie Rapaport, Jill Carle, Marshall Garland, and Anna Saavedra, "Students' Civic Online Reasoning: A National Portrait," *Educational Researcher*, 50, no. 8 (2021): 505–515.
13. Korona, Matthew, and Dawn Hathaway, "Visual Literacy in Teacher Education: Examining the Complexity of Online Images for Instructional and Personal Purposes," *Journal of Technology and Teacher Education*, 29, no. 4 (2021): 533–557.

https://search.ebscohost.com/login.aspx?direct=true&db=eric&AN=EJ1334893 &site=ehost-live https://learntechlib.org/primary/p/219934/.

14. Brown, Nicole, Kaila Bussert, Denise Hattwig, and Ann Medaille, *Visual Literacy for Libraries: A Practical, Standards-Based Guide*. Chicago, IL: ALA Editions, an imprint of the American Library Association, 2016.

15. Moline, Steve, *I See what You Mean: Visual Literacy, K-8. Second Edition*. New York: Stenhouse Publishers 2011.

10

Multicultural and Cultural Literacy in K–12

Ewa Dziedzic-Elliot, School of Education Subject Librarian, The College of New Jersey, New Jersey

Before taking a deep look at multicultural and cultural literacies, we need to establish a basic level of understanding of what they are. For the purpose of this chapter, I will attempt to define these terms while taking into consideration many facets. In no way will it be a final and only definition, but rather an opening to a conversation about the complexity of the issue, aiming to capture the essence of multicultural and cultural education through information literacy in a school library or a classroom.

Multicultural and cultural literacies are multidisciplinary concepts that provide historical, sociological, literary, artistic, ethnographic, and educational contexts that bleed into school librarianship. This list can be expanded to other disciplines depending on the context and perspective. Both terms can be used to describe a big picture on a national or ethnic level, or quite the opposite within a local community or group.

Cultural literacy is when one is able to adapt the cues from their own background and lived experiences and use them correctly in social situations. We associate culture with race, ethnicity, heritage, language, food, dress code, and body language, but there are also societal groups that have their own culture within the larger body of culture. Culture can often be viewed through the lens of stereotypes and biases deeply rooted in our own perspectives of the world around us. We all have an image in our head when we think about a culture from an X country or Y city, or Z profession. By acknowledging and understanding our own stereotypes and biases, analyzing, and taking them apart, we learn how to deal with them in our personal and professional lives.

Multicultural literacy is when one is able to follow cultural cues and understand that there are other acceptable behaviors that might feel foreign to them. The two terms that are included refer to many cultures within the community or societal group with the ability to be literate and able to "read it." American multicultural literacy is unique, representing contexts that are specific to this country, its history, or evolution and growth; therefore, looking at this concept has to be more local.

American multicultural education encompasses all student groups (or subgroups) that include nationality, race, ethnicity, language, religion, gender identification, sexual orientation, and more. Within the larger multicultural group, we recognize further cultural components that include various household environments, such as urban vs. suburban, parental/legal guardian presence, socioeconomic status, language proficiencies, educational background, or heritage.

The term "multiculturalism" is often limited to race or ethnicity. In my opinion, this is a limiting factor to a much broader and deeper concept that includes layers of multiculturalism, such as language, faith, or ancestry and their interconnectedness.

American demographics change state by state and even within the state. Some states have robust international, foreign-born populations, while some are made up of what is considered to be multigenerational American-born people.

Weil writes about the concept of three underlying tenets of a Critical Multicultural Literacy: educational equity, prejudice reduction, and creating opportunities for fair-minded critical thinking within different cultural points of view on contemporary and historical issues.[1] In his article, he writes that the way we typically approach multicultural literacy is harmful and can only further strengthen existing biases and stereotypes. Although I agree with this point, I disagree with calling American education a Eurocentric education and would propose that it would be better referred to as an Anglocentric education. We would have Eurocentric education if we taught European languages at the level of bilingual schools or if we taught European history, geography, or literature. Instead, we teach all of these subjects selectively, focusing on the British influence upon the United States' evolution from a historical and literary perspective. When I walked into my previous high school library and looked at the nonfiction section, I was very surprised to see that two-thirds or more of the critical literary works were on Shakespeare. Where is Zola, Nabokov, Proust, or Goethe?

Taylor and Hoechsmann, in their article, call for a multicultural literacy curriculum as the best way to address racial inequalities and racism especially "in the areas of low ethnoracial and linguistic diversity."[2] In their study, students with multilingual backgrounds scored higher on their historical and factual global knowledge. The authors claim that "school represents the most important as well as consistent source of multicultural literacy."[3]

Garcia-Mila et al. published an article that evaluated structured dialogic teaching techniques among preschool, elementary, and secondary students. Based on their findings, they stated that their strategy "was effective in helping children and adolescents to overcome pre-existing stereotypes and prejudices

(. . .)."[4] The dialogic practice as a pedagogical method that expands the traditional concept of cultural literacy is also elaborated in an article written by Maine et al. Authors implicate that the best practice is to move away from thinking about cultural literacy as a "knowledge of culture" and toward seeing it as "dialogic practice enabled through constructive encounters about what it means to be different from each other."[5]

In this chapter, I will acknowledge that there is an aspect of multicultural literacy that highlights student groups that were born in other countries or had parents who were born elsewhere in the world, and how that impacts the multicultural aspect of the local schools.[6]

Although not every region of the United States will have students who are bilingual and actively practice customs from abroad, it is important to plant the seed of tolerance and acceptance in others during the early ages of education of our students. As parents, we don't raise our children to stay with us forever; we instead raise them to be young, independent individuals who become active participants in a global society. As educators, and especially school librarians, we don't teach them to limit their perspectives. We instead want to stimulate their growth, support their natural curiosity, and provide them with tools adequate to their learning.

Depending on the part of the country where we teach, this concept is going to be crucial for school librarians to understand. We cannot look at the body of our students the same way across the country since our demographics, audience, and local communities change, and the needs for multicultural literacy change as well.

In this chapter, I will use the term "authentic learning" to mean a type of learning based on educational experiences that introduce critical thinking, the ability to analyze information, and learning through exposure without strengthening stereotypes and biases. An excellent example of authentic learning is described by Matuk and Rugierello, who created a Culture Connection Project: a study that showed the effectiveness of teaching multiculturalism through drama.[7] Teaching multicultural literacy through acting may remind one of the ancient Greek concept of catharsis, which allowed the performers and audience to share feelings of happiness or sorrow, and to experience an emotional cleanse.

BEST STORIES ARE PERSONAL STORIES

Foreign-born parents often don't speak their mother tongue to their children to ensure that their child will not have issues in an English-speaking environment. There are a lot of misconceptions about delayed speech and learning if a child is bilingual, equating code-switching to a developmental language disorder.[8]

Reading Hamel and Barger[9] brought me back to the times when my son was attending his Polish daycare. Just like Spanish-speaking children in the article, he was surrounded by his peers speaking both languages, being introduced to the stories, history, geography, traditions, and food from his mother's homeland.

We had a lot of concerns when he went to an American school regarding his Polish language skills but also his sense of belonging in the Polish culture. Will he still be interested in reading Polish books during his bedtime? Will he speak and understand what is spoken to him? Is he going to continue to eat his Polish food? Will he be interested in staying in touch with his non-English-speaking cousins? Will he be proud of his visits to Poland?

I am using my family experience as an example because where we live in New Jersey, this is not an unusual situation. 71.6 percent of students in New Jersey spoke English in the 2021–22 school year; 17.6 percent of them spoke Spanish; and 9.7 percent spoke other languages.[10] More than a quarter of the students in the state spoke languages other than English.

MULTICULTURAL LITERACY IN EARLY EDUCATION

Not every student sitting in front of us went to a daycare and learned how to interact with and make new friends outside of home. For some of our students, coming to Pre-K might be their first contact with a school-like environment that provides structure, expectations, a daily routine, and new classmates.

The first clues to getting to know their new friends are through their senses. Vision: do they look like me? Do they dress like me? Do they look different? Smell: do they smell like me? Does their food smell like mine? Why do they smell different? Auditory: do they speak like me? Why or why not? Touch: can I hold their hand? Can I tackle them? Why can't I tackle them? Taste: Why is their food so weird?

Those of us who have worked with younger children know that they will not only assess their surroundings, but they will also be very vocal about their discoveries. Our job is to teach our very young friends that we are not the same and that this circumstance is normal. They need to be taught at a very young age that there is nothing wrong with being dressed differently, having different haircuts, or head coverings. Some of us smell different because of the cultural things we do at home, like cooking pungent food or using incense for religious purposes. Some of us speak with funny-sounding accents because English is not our first language, and we have the "superpower" of being able to communicate in another language. Eventually, through their observations and our modeling, our friends will understand that our differences are beautiful and make us who we are.

As school librarians, we can do that through introductions to appropriate early-childhood literature. Through careful selection of our materials, we can teach acceptance and tolerance. Careless use of literary materials can be harmful if used to promote or support superstitions and biased stereotypes.

AUTHENTIC MULTICULTURAL ACTIVITIES FOR EARLY ELEMENTARY

Add interactive, non-lecturing hands-on activities to allow students to become experts in sharing their own knowledge about their cultural experiences and to build a multicultural space. Add a concept of which facets of cultures they are familiar with and what they are interested in learning.

A very simple activity you can bring into your space is using greetings from around the world. If you have students who can become teachers for a moment, let them. If your class is not very diverse, use technology and look up greetings in other languages. You can turn this into a regular activity by designating a day in which students vote for which language they will use to greet each other. Create a quick lesson about the greeting and the country. It doesn't have to be very complex. Keep things simple for your young learners; for example, this week we are greeting one another in French. To allow authentic learning that does not strengthen common stereotypes, give them a real fun fact about the country: the French flag is blue, white, and red. Do you know any other countries that have those same colors in their flag?[11]

I would not recommend talking about travel as an example of teaching multicultural literacy since not all of our students and their families might have the same opportunities to exercise that form of learning.

Of course, one of the easiest choices for school librarians is to select early elementary books to teach multicultural literacy. The American Library Association annual awards can be a great way to start building a strong multicultural collection by using, for example, the Mildred L. Batchelder Award for books in languages other than English.[12]

AUTHENTIC MULTICULTURAL ACTIVITIES FOR ELEMENTARY GRADES

As with any other skills, multicultural literacy has to be scaffolded based on the students' learning abilities and readiness. At this stage of their academic growth, we will be introducing more complex language and learning tools and activities. In some of our schools, students will have access to subscription-paid databases that are excellent tech tools and provide two types of learning: the mechanical skills of using a device and the content that it can provide.[13]

Before diving into developing multicultural literacy programs, one needs to get to know their district and school culture. The educator or librarian needs to have a deep understanding of what kinds of activities will be welcome and which ones will make the local community uncomfortable. If you have a diverse community that is very active in the school's life, it will be appropriate to invite guests to your classroom for a day of authentic learning. They can teach your students how to perform a national dance, sing a song in their language, or create an artistic decoration typical for a specific holiday.

In one of the elementary schools where I worked, we held an annual International Food Festival. It was an afterschool activity in which parents signed up to bring food samples and created posters and activities related to their home countries. The whole school was invited to participate in the activity. Our students proudly shared their favorite delicacies, recipes, cultural games, and trivia about their culture. An event of that caliber not only serves as a vehicle to strengthen students' love of their heritage, but it also allows their parents to become part of the school's community. It enables educators to get a glimpse of the family structure, the level of support, and observe the customs and traditions of the students in their class. In some of those communities, it is not uncommon for parents to come wearing traditional clothing, accompanied by their extended families and not just their immediate family unit composed of parents and children.

Upper elementary grades often work on projects about other countries. In the past, the approach was to talk about personal heritage, which might not be very equitable. If one thinks about the involuntary conditions under which some community members came to the United States or those whose ancestors came here centuries ago, many students may be too far removed from their places of origin. Also, some family histories carry a lot of pain and generational trauma. Instead, use a learning approach that focuses on the cultures, places, customs, foods, and languages that the students are curious about. Places that mean something to us, that we read about, watched a movie about, and want to explore more.

One of my favorite duties as a librarian is creating multidisciplinary activities that bring together reading/writing skills, visual and performing arts, history, or geography. Select a book that introduces another culture and let the story inspire you to create a meaningful activity around it. In New Jersey, we introduce fairy tales to students around the second grade. What a great teaching opportunity for authentic learning. I know that we often select modern, less gruesome versions of the tales, but we have an opportunity to tap into the origins of the stories, mention the nationality of the creators, and talk about their historical periods. Since the text might be too much, maybe we can show the older illustrations from the original fairy tales? And who says we need to go with Brothers Grimm or Hans Christian Andersen? We can use fairy tales and stories of origin from around the world.

Another interesting activity for elementary-age students is giving them "passports" and having them visit countries around the world through books and digital tools. Students collect stamps in their passports after "visiting" other countries. Of course, there is a form that allows students to keep track of their newly acquired knowledge. This is an especially useful activity in those states where learning about other countries is part of the state standards.

AUTHENTIC MULTICULTURAL ACTIVITIES FOR MIDDLE GRADES

Sixth–eighth graders can be more aware of how they learn best. School librarians can support the love of other languages, curiosity about other cultures and traditions, and how they are tied to the concept of humanity on a global level. The school library can provide the environment for that level of multicultural literacy exploration.

Middle school is a big challenge for many learners since they are not children anymore, yet they are not teens either. Some are more ready than others to exercise their independence, and some struggle with it. Independence from their loved ones, independence from their childhood friends, and independence from past habits cause a lot of tension, anxiety, and stress. This is when their exploration of self becomes increasingly more visible.

School librarians with appropriate amounts of instruction time and resources can set students on the path of discovery and true lifelong learning.

One of the most successful middle school library programs I have seen was the creation of a museum exhibit. During an annual celebration, students at the school were given a task: choose an object, learn about the person who created it, and prepare a museum-like display with important facts about the object and creator. We can add a multicultural aspect: find an object created by a person from a specific country/cultural background to create your display. When the pieces are done, organize an exhibition showcasing the multicultural artifacts. You can take this concept one step further and create a live museum: students select a role model, learn interesting facts about them, and dress up as them. During the exhibition, the displayed "statues" come to life and recite what they have learned.[14]

Because of the advantages of our digital world, we can also create virtual international school library visits. Several years ago, I reached out to my high school friends from Poland who live throughout the world, and my students had an opportunity to talk to them about Poland, their professional lives, personal hobbies, and international education. If you don't have anybody who can open this window of opportunity, partner up with the world language department in your school. You can create programs that would support their foreign language skills but also multicultural literacy.

It is very appropriate to start having educator/librarian-guided conversations about difficult topics and for the school library to provide developmentally appropriate materials that support students' authentic learning. It is crucial for students to establish research habits that will teach them about the evaluation of resources, both academic and nonacademic, driven by their need to learn. It is most important for students to be taught critical thinking skills that will allow them not only to communicate information but allow them to question, dissect, and analyze what is in front of them.

AUTHENTIC MULTICULTURAL ACTIVITIES FOR HIGH SCHOOL

When working in high school, I noticed that adults often assume that students learned or should have learned something in previous years and overestimate their knowledge. This includes social cues and competencies. The situation became even more visible after students spent a significant amount of time in isolation during COVID-19.

The conversation about culture and multiculturalism in high school looks different from previous years. Teens learn to navigate which part of their cultural background they would like to share or reveal and what they need to conceal because it is not socially acceptable in a mainstream American high school. Many high schoolers live in two worlds: the home world with one set of norms and the school world with a very different set of norms. That might include language, food, dress code, ability to socialize with friends after school, nonacademic activities, and extracurricular activities that focus on culture and heritage, etc.

Interacting with teens who are willing to share and open up about their culture is the most rewarding experience any school librarian can dream of. All the years empowering and encouraging students to become master teachers and mentors come to fruition.

As always, collaboration with other educators is key, especially in art, music, or culinary arts. Here is how these unusual connections with teachers and students became an integral part of my high school library:

1. Art: students made pisanki[15] in an art class and displayed them in the library.
2. Music: The choir teacher worked on a piece in Polish. I assisted her in finding notes and proper pronunciation of the words. The choir performed the piece in the library during a busy lunch break, earning a standing ovation from the audience. Later, the song was included in their holiday concert. It melted my heart and the hearts of all the other community members who have Polish roots (about 5 percent of our local community).

I know that one of the easiest activities is to create bulletin boards. In my high school library, we turned a bulletin board into an authentic and interactive learning experience.

Example #1: One of my favorite bulletin boards we have ever made was one for Asian American and Pacific Islander Heritage Month. We created a map of Asia and printed a sample of book covers of Asian authors, books with Asian protagonists, or books with plots relating to that part of the world. Then we connected the printed book cover page with a string to the respective country. The board drew a lot of attention. Students were interested in discovering who wrote what and how it related to a specific country. They were not shy to admit learning some basic geographical facts, such as Russia is in Europe and Asia.

Figure 10.1 Bulletin Board with the Map of Asia. *Source:* Ewa Dziedzic-Elliott.

Example #2: During my time working in high school, one of the most powerful initiatives that we created in the library was a stand against the war in Ukraine when it first broke out in spring 2022. Our school has a significant Eastern European population of students from Ukraine, Russia, Belarus, and Poland. Students came to me saying: Our American-born friends don't understand what is happening, why it is happening, and why we are upset. They make inappropriate and insensitive jokes. Can we do something about it?'

So we did.

Using our bulletin board space, we created a blue and yellow flag where everyone at school could come and sign a pledge against the war in Ukraine. Some of them were written in English, but several were written in foreign languages. It was a good thing that the librarian (me) was able to read Cyrillic in order to ensure that only appropriate language was being used.

We also created a fundraiser by selling blue and yellow ribbons and sent the profits to a Ukrainian organization supporting war-stricken communities. Most importantly, we hosted a series of lectures and talks led by Eastern European students. The students created the content using their knowledge from their weekend foreign language schools, prepared well-researched and well-cited presentations, stood in front of their teachers, school administrators, and friends, and allowed themselves to be the teachers. One of the proudest moments of my career as a school librarian was seeing my usually quiet students—many of them speaking with an accent—stand in front of a large audience to teach others. They communicated what it meant to them hearing that bombs fell only a few hours away from their hometowns, their parents' hometowns, their grandparents' homes, or places they had lived or visited. Students allowed themselves to

Figure 10.2 Ukrainian Flag with Pledges against War in Ukraine. *Source:* Ewa Dziedzic-Elliott.

be honest yet respectful instructors, knowledgeable, willing to learn and teach, and proud and humble all at the same time. The adults and students in the audience asked appropriate questions, shared their own stories, and most importantly, created a safe space for vulnerable and authentic learning.

FINAL WORD

Why do cultural and multicultural literacies matter? Because they teach tolerance, respect for others who are different, broaden the students' spectrum, and prepare them for adult life. We live in a multicultural global world. If we think that these concepts are new, we are very wrong. During the Enlightenment period (1685–1815), there was a widely used concept of cosmopolitanism that highlighted the idea of being a citizen of the world. One who fluently speaks multiple languages, extensively travels, and is aware of modern trends in arts, fashion, and literature. During that time, there were no planes or technology that supported instantaneous cross-continental communication, and there wasn't even medicine that would allow safe migrations from one region of the world to another.

We ought to use our library resources to ensure that our students are ready for the world that once used to feel exceptionally large.

In case you were sitting at the edge of the chair wondering how my son is doing in American school, he found his people there. Many of his friends have parents from other countries. Children teach each other phrases in their languages, share stories about their traditions and customs, and bring ethnic snacks. His school provides a safe space for multilingual and multicultural children, teaching them to be proud of their otherness and to not be ashamed of it.

NOTES

1. Danny Weil, "Towards a Critical Multicultural Literacy: Advancing an Education for Liberation," *Roeper Review* 15 (4) (1993): 211, https://search.ebscohost.com/login .aspx?direct=true&db=aph&AN=9511241479&site=ehost-live.
2. Lisa Taylor and Michael Hoechsmann, "Why Multicultural Literacy? Multicultural Education Inside and Outside Schools," in *Precarious International Multicultural Education*, 315–332. Rotterdam: SensePublishers, 2011.
3. Lisa Taylor and Michael Hoechsmann. "Why Multicultural Literacy? Multicultural Education Inside and Outside Schools." In *Precarious International Multicultural Education*, 315–332. Rotterdam: SensePublishers, 2011.
4. Merce Garcia-Mila, Andrea Miralda-Banda, Jose Luna, Ana Remesal, Núria Castells, and Sandra Gilabert, "Change in Classroom Dialogicity to Promote Cultural Literacy Across Educational Levels," *Sustainability* 13 (11) (June 1, 2021), https://search.pro-quest.com/docview/2539992801.
5. Fiona Maine, Victoria Cook, and Tuuli Lähdesmäki, "Reconceptualizing Cultural Literacy as a Dialogic Practice," *London Review of Education* 17 (3) (November 1, 2019), https://search.proquest.com/docview/2314650504.
6. Author's note: During my preparation to write this chapter, I noticed a trend: American library scholars focus on information literacy in relation to the Association of College and Research Libraries framework, writing about its implementation and impact on higher education or focusing on specific types of information literacy such as data, tech, and media literacies. Unfortunately, the subjects of cultural and multicultural literacies are not as well-covered, especially in recent years. The author of this chapter selected articles from various parts of the world that were the closest to reflecting concepts and principles that align with American realities.
7. Lucia Yiu Matuk and Tina Ruggirello, "Culture Connection Project: Promoting Multi-culturalism in Elementary Schools," *Canadian Journal of Public Health* 1 (98) (2007): 26–29, https://doi.org/10.1007/bf03405380.
8. Several studies show that there are no significant differences between code-switching related to developmental language disorder (DLD) or typical language development: "therefore, the frequency and type of code-switches should not be used as an indicator of DLD." See: Maria Kapantzoglou, Julie Esparza Brown, Lauren Cycyk, and Gerasimos Fergadiotis, "Code-Switching and Language Proficiency in Bilingual Children with and without Developmental Language Disorder," *Journal of Speech, Language, and Hearing Research, JSLHR* 64 (5) (May 11, 2021): 1605–1620.

9. Erin Hamel and Bettie Parsons Barger, "Reimagining Resources: Creating Spaces that Explore Multicultural Literacies," *School-University Partnerships* 15 (2) (Summer 2022): 80–87, https://ezproxy.tcnj.edu/login?url=https://www.proquest.com/scholarly-journals/reimagining-resources-creating-spaces-that/docview/2712291343/se-2.

10. "New Jersey State Report 2021–22," Official Site of the State of New Jersey, https://rc.doe.state.nj.us/2021-2022/state/detail/demographics?lang=EN.

11. There are many reputable educational free resources that can be used here, for example: National Geographic Kids: https://kids.nationalgeographic.com/, PBS Learning Media for Teachers: https://whyy.pbslearningmedia.org/, or BBC Teach: https://www.bbc.co.uk/teach.

12. "American Library Association Announces 2024 Youth Media Award Winners," https://www.ala.org/news/press-releases/2024/01/american-library-association-announces-2024-youth-media-award-winners. Another resource worth checking for New Jersey educators might be the Rutgers International Youth Literature Collection, which holds children's books from around the world: https://sites.rutgers.edu/iyc/iylc/.

13. Please see other chapters of this book that refer to tech and digital literacies.

14. These ideas are inspired by two educators: Lisa Hall and Eileen Cramer, both from Lawrence Township Public Schools in New Jersey.

15. Description of Pisanki from https://culture.pl/en/article/discover-the-world-of-pisanki-or-polish-easter-eggs.

11

How Images Manipulate Us

Robbie Barber, Teacher-Librarian, Tucker High School, Georgia

We are constantly bombarded with composed images, from billboards, commercials, and magazine advertisements to a plethora of social media images. The images fly by almost too quickly to interpret what you saw. All these images are designed to evoke a response from the viewer. Teaching visual literacy to students requires reviewing how other images are manipulated. The manipulations can be used to create desire for a product, or to support or abandon a person, organization, political party, or charity. When you look at an image, how did it make you feel?

For example, look at the image of the flower in figure 11.1.[1]

Figure 11.1 Pretty Flower. *Source*: Photo/Perduejn, CC By 3.0, via Wikimedia Commons.

Figure 11.2 Weird flower. *Source*: Photo/Perduejn, CC By 3.0, via Wikimedia Commons.

Think about your emotions when viewing the image of a flower. Does it make you smile or feel good for the moment?

Now look at the next image, figure 11.2.[2]

What emotions roll through you when you look at the second flower? Do you feel anxious or negative emotions?

Stop and think for a moment. Did I manipulate you with images and words? Absolutely. First, I showed you a normal-looking flower. Then, I showed the odd-looking one. The order mattered. Because the flowers were shown in a specific order, it implies something different than if you had only seen one image. Further, I specifically asked if you had negative emotions. Simply using words implying that you might have negative emotions may bring those emotions out.

In reality, these two flowers (figure 11.3[3]) are the same type, and the odd-looking one is called "fascination," which occurs naturally for a variety of reasons in nature.[4] The same plant may have a "fascination" during one growth period and appear normal the following year.[5]

According to Casas and Williams (2019), images that evoke enthusiasm, anger, or fear mobilize people to react and share with others about the image. Images that evoke sadness translate to people doing less with engagement or sharing.[6] But, Hou et al. (2023) found that images evoking sadness or

Figure 11.3 Fascination flowers. *Source:* Photo/Perduejn, CC By 3.0, via Wikimedia Commons.

contentment garnered more donations for public crowdfunding projects.[7] This means that our emotional reaction to images can affect how much money we share, how we engage or disengage with others, and how we address other issues including social and political ones.

To handle our reactions to images, we need to learn to recognize our emotional reactions. Some items may cause us to have an emotional, knee-jerk reaction. An emotional, knee-jerk reaction is when you respond to a stimulus without thought. It feels automatic. The solution to handling your emotions and these unexpected knee-jerk reactions is to train yourself to do one thing: Pause.

INTENTIONALITY MATTERS

Understanding keywords is important in understanding how images create an emotional reaction. **Mis**information is generally referred to as someone posting false information without being aware that it is false. The "mis-" prefix means wrong or mistaken. **Dis**information is posting false information on purpose, generally with the intent to cause harm to others. The "dis-" prefix means the opposite. Some create disinformation to forward their own beliefs. Others do so to make money or create havoc. **Mal**information is posting truthful information in such a way to create harm.[8] The "mal-" prefix means bad. A person may release true information about another person that is taken out of context or it may be something that making public at this particular moment makes it harmful.

The key to these three words is understanding the intent of the person sharing. The reality is that misinformation cannot always be distinguished, despite the fact that there is no intent to lie or lead you astray. The overlap between misinformation, disinformation, and malinformation can cover a wide body of social media postings. Try looking up a political posting on a social media site. Create a list of questions that may help you verify the content. For example, you can ask:

- Is it completely true?
- Is it partially true?
- Is it false?
- Does it intend harm?
- Can you defend your position by proving that information?

To handle the array of questions that occur, just pause and let yourself ask and answer the tumult of issues.

MANIPULATION TOOLS

How do others create images that move us? Let's look at four popular methods: Camera angles, backgrounds, cropping, and captions. The angle may manipulate emotions by highlighting features and hiding others. Backgrounds may create a softening feeling or the horror of war. Cropping an image to prevent you from gaining the full understanding of the situation of the image. Combining an image with words will change how the observer interprets the image.

The next picture is an example of a camera angle and a little cropping that changes the entire concept of a picture.

On a hot summer's day, I took a walk in the city. I saw a dog and took a picture. Depending on the cropping, you see two entirely different stories with the dog. In figure 11.4,[9] the story is simply a dog on an outside walk on a hot day. If we look at the uncropped image in figure 11.5,[10] the story changes and you can see why I stopped and took the picture in the first place.

This is a simple picture taken with a smartphone. Using a standard cropping tool, with no other modifications to the image, I changed the story.

Captioning changes your emotional pull. In figure 11.6,[11] the dog is baring his teeth and the caption implies danger. There is no background to provide a context and no other information available. Emotionally, there may be a feeling of pulling back to be safe. In figure 11.7,[12] the background shows a person's hand and maybe a piece of couch. The caption is a soft font with a soft blue, and implies the dog is merely tired and perhaps startled.

Robbie Barber

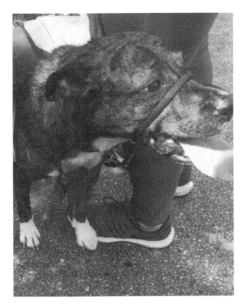

Figure 11.4 Dog on a Walk. *Source*: Robbie Barber.

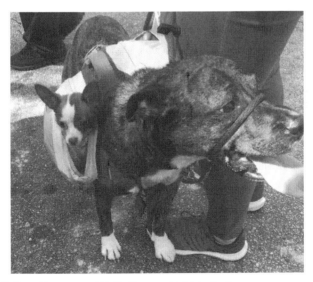

Figure 11.5 Two Dogs on a Walk. *Source*: Robbie Barber.

Figure 11.6 Scary Dog. *Source*: Robbie Barber.

Figure 11.7 Startled Dog on the Sofa. *Source*: Robbie Barber.

For an exercise, print a picture from social media or the newspaper of war or protests of war. Ask some questions to see what students can interpret without seeing the article linked to the image. Questions may include:

- What emotion do you feel when you look at the picture? Are you encouraged or horrified?
- What is missing in the image?
- What changes if you cut off part of the image?
- What is the picture designed to do?
- What if you removed the caption or changed it? If the caption of a person holding a gun is "Rebel," do you feel differently than if the caption is "Terrorist?"
- What if the background was changed?
- Which political party does this support? Why?

You can have students create their own questions based on the image. Once again, the trick to handling image evaluation is to pause and allow your brain to analyze rather than react to the image.

REVERSE IMAGE SEARCH

Now that you have created several questions, what else can you do? The best thing is to try to learn more about the image itself. Using a reverse image search, students can use their internet browser to search for more information and articles on the image. Students can use TinEye (https://tineye.com/) to reverse image search by uploading the image to the browser. When you upload the fascination flowers, there are several articles including a Snopes source and a Global News source. Another source is using Chrome's reverse image search. You can upload the image to Chrome's image page (https://images .google.com/) or you can use your smartphone's Chrome. On your phone, find an image in Chrome and click and hold. One option that shows up is to Search Images with Chrome. You can also use the Google Lens app to do the same. Again, you will get a list of options and information. This provides you an opportunity to reevaluate the image and other items it matches.

WHY PRACTICE?

In every section of this chapter, there is a suggestion to practice looking at images and interpreting their intent. But why all the practice? After all, everyone is constantly bombarded with images from billboards, TV shows, and social media. We are surrounded by images. Do we need to practice more? According to Shen et al. (2018), the more a person experiences evaluating images, the better they get at correctly interpreting the image's credibility.[13] This means building skills over time. Rather than trying it on your own, several reputable organizations provide a safe method of practicing with students.

The News Literacy Project (https://newslit.org/) is a nonpartisan, educational nonprofit that advances the idea of improving news literacy throughout American society. The News Literacy Project (NLP) provides educators with materials, webinars, and podcasts to help teach news literacy. One of the NLP tools is Checkology©, a browser-based software intended for sixth through twelfth graders to practice news literacy. NLP also started RumorGuard (https://www.rumorguard.org/) to provide images and explanations of various social media disinformation. Another organization, the National Association for Media Literacy Education, also provides webinars and education for educators. Membership for educators is free and you can choose to receive information.

Practicing with images and evaluating them may feel clunky at first. It takes practice. Students working together in groups will be faster at questioning and analyzing the image. The more familiar the process of evaluating images, the more successful the student will be in recognizing, questioning, and understanding when they are being manipulated. After all, a picture can convey an idea, information, and a strong emotion in an instant.

NOTES

1. Perduejn, CC BY 3.0. https://creativecommons.org/licenses/by/3.0, via Wikimedia Commons.
2. Ibid.
3. Ibid.
4. Fessenden, Maris. "Don't Freak Out Over the Funky Flowers That Appeared Near Fukushima." *Smithsonian Magazine*, July 24, 2015. https://www.smithsonianmag.com/smart-news/dont-freak-out-over-funky-flowers-appeared-near-fukushima-180956021/.
5. Ibid.
6. Casas, Andreu, and Nora Webb Williams. "Images That Matter: Online Protests and the Mobilizing Role of Pictures." *Political Research Quarterly*, 72, no. 2 (2019): 360–375. http://www.jstor.org/stable/45276914.
7. Hou, Jian-Ren, Jie Zhang, and Kunpeng Zhang. "Pictures That Are Worth a Thousand Donations: How Emotions in Project Images Drive the Success of Online Charity Fundraising Campaigns? An Image Design Perspective." *MIS Quarterly*, 47, no. 2 (2020): 535–583. https://doi.org/10.25300/MISQ/2022/17164.
8. Greene, Jim, "Malinformation." Salem Press Encyclopedia, April 2023. https://research.ebsco.com/linkprocessor/plink?id=c354e086-3a52-357a-9168-e8eca663a3c9.
9. Barber, Robbie. 2019. CC BY 4.0. http://creativecommons.org/licenses/by/4.0/.
10. Ibid.
11. Barber. 2023. CC BY 4.0. http://creativecommons.org/licenses/by/4.0/.
12. Ibid.
13. Shen, Cuihua, Mona Kasra, Wenjing Pan, Grace A Bassett, Yining Malloch, and James F. O'Brien. "Fake Images: The Effects of Source, Intermediary, and Digital Media Literacy on Contextual Assessment of Image Credibility Online." *New Media & Society*, 21, no. 2 (2018): 438–463. https://doi.org/10.1177/1461444818799526.

12

Developing Information Literacy Habits for College and Beyond

Holly Weimar, Library Science Professor and Chair of the Department of Library Science and Technology, Sam Houston State University, Texas; Elizabeth Gross, Associate Professor of Library Science and Technology, Sam Houston State University, Texas; and, Ashley B. Crane, Assistant Professor and Research and Instruction Librarian at Sam Houston State University, Texas

Information literacy (IL) is many things. Digital literacy, media literacy, and research as inquiry are just some of the main facets. Students come to higher education with varying experiences of library instruction. Not all students have the same experiences or skill sets to utilize the university library. The university library itself may also be an unknown entity, even for those familiar with libraries in general. After arriving on campus, students may not utilize the campus library, even though there are many portals to assist them, such as chat, email, direct conversation, and subject-specific content management systems. They may not be aware of or may not know how to access these resources. Professors ask academic librarians to explain these important resources to students, and they are available to the students for any and all queries. Sometimes the librarian is embedded within the course, but many times librarians are asked to perform a "one shot" to help students figure out how to navigate the university library. The professors themselves may also need support in the use of the library to meet their own information needs as well as those of their students.

The Association of College and Research Libraries (ACRL) recognizes the need for information literacy support as a continuum from K–12 education, as outlined by the American Association of School Librarians. ACRL's information literacy competency framework shows the importance of this continuum:

Information Literacy Competency Standards for Higher Education ... extends the work of the American Association of School Librarians Task Force on Information Literacy Standards, thereby providing higher education an opportunity to articulate its information literacy competencies with those of K-12 so that a continuum of expectations develops for students at all levels.[1]

The notion of information literacy includes the following behaviors: "Learning to find information, learning techniques, applying learning, building knowledge and understanding, and learning about professional practice."[2] Although university-level information literacy seems to be an endpoint, the application of the techniques and understanding of the use and application of information is a lifelong practice. Formally, these begin at the K–12 level and are built upon as students grow and mature in their ability to apply the skills.

The definition of information literacy, as outlined by the ACRL, is "the set of integrated abilities encompassing the reflective discovery of information, the understanding of how information is produced and valued, and the use of information in creating new knowledge and ethically participating in communities of learning."[3] The many facets of information-seeking and critical analysis of what is found can begin in K–12. Students may not have the neural maturity to understand all the procedures necessary to successfully achieve this goal at all levels.

However, school librarians are responsible for laying the groundwork for students. Information comes from many different sources and angles. It is important to be able to discern credible from bogus information. IL instruction can help instill those skills that ultimately lead to critical thinking and ethical evaluation of information. The result is a society of lifelong learners who are equipped with the tools and skills to be thoughtful and canny information consumers.

In the following, we unpack these notions and show how school librarians can help students prepare for college success. The skills and mindset inculcated by the school librarian's instruction in IL will help students be more comfortable with search and retrieval, and will help them create products that represent their learning.

INFORMATION LITERACY IN COLLEGE

From the very first day a learner decides to pursue a college education, they are inundated with information. They are expected to sift through an overwhelming amount of print, electronic, and verbal information about different colleges and universities, their academic offerings and rankings, their support services, and even social opportunities to make an informed decision on where to go and

Holly A. Weimar, Elizabeth A. Gross, and Ashley B. Crane

what their path will be when they get there. It doesn't stop once that decision is made; students will continue to have a vast amount of information thrown at and available to them from Welcome Week to graduation.

This information overload goes beyond the classroom as college forces students, often for the first time, to experience what it is like to be an adult in a new environment. Students may be figuring out how to do their own laundry, discovering how to take care of themselves during an illness, or how to balance homework and dependent schedules all while discovering how they learn best, what study strategies work for them, and navigating the unwritten norms of college life. A student's success depends on how well they can recognize a need for information, navigate the information environment, evaluate the information they find, and apply it to their situation in the midst of new living and academic environments, added stressors, and changing identities and relationships.

Everything a college student needs is available in the library, right? Maybe ... but what if they never get there? Over three decades of research has shown that many college students experience library anxiety, a feeling that other students are competent at using the library while they alone are incompetent and that this lack of competence is shameful and must be hidden.[4,5] Most commonly, this feeling prevents college students from seeking help from academic library staff or librarians but may also prevent students from even walking in the door in fear that they may be seen using the library wrong.

Library anxiety can be exacerbated by outside influences including socioeconomic factors, procrastination, and perfectionism.[6,7,8] College students coming from lower socioeconomic backgrounds generally have limited experience with libraries and academic research.[9] They may not know that help can be had or how to go about asking for it.[10] Students who procrastinate or are struggling with other aspects of college life also experience increased levels of library anxiety.[11,12] The opposite is also true, that those students who believe that others are expecting them to be perfect also experience higher rates of library anxiety.[13]

Students are known to consider their information literacy skills to be sufficient to meet of the needs of their coursework by the time they enter college, perhaps as a way to protect themselves from the shame aspect of library anxiety,[14] though research has shown that students consistently overestimate their information literacy skills.[15] This overestimation, combined with a need for convenience, connection, and familiarity, leads college students to limit their search for information to known search engines, databases, and resources.[16,17] In using tools like Google, Wikipedia, and JSTOR, college students have created a sense of comfort by learning how to use the tools, the kinds of information that will be pulled, and their quality level.[18]

INFORMATION LITERACY AND PRESERVICE TEACHERS

While students entering college know that they have some information literacy skills, few recognize how that knowledge will be used as professionals within their chosen field. Students who have chosen to major or minor in Education with the hope of becoming K–12 teacher are often shocked to find that they will be expected to not only break down research into reasonable chunks and apply it to their teaching, but also teach information literacy concepts and skills in digestible and grade-level appropriate ways to their K–12 students to aid in their academic success. Because a student's level of information literacy is closely tied to their teacher's,[19] it is important that preservice teachers be exposed to and build their own information literacy throughout their college experience.

Information literacy generally isn't the focus of a single course; instead, these preservice teachers are expected to pick it up along the way through instances found in several courses, such as literacy or technology integration, that are often already overloaded with content. Adding to the confusion, these courses may focus primarily on media, digital, or technology literacy[20,21] without presenting their connections to information literacy. As often happens in Education courses, preservice teachers are asked to consider the concept behind the skill more deeply and from different perspectives, which forces them to question their understanding of a topic and leads to an uncertainty in the preservice teachers' ability to be an authority on that concept. Ranschaert found this to be true even following three semesters of targeted, specific media literacy intervention.[22]

PREPARING LEARNERS FOR THE DEMANDS OF COLLEGE

The varied school IL experiences that preservice teachers had prior to arriving at university may require added support from their academic librarians to help them become proficient in IL. Looking back on their possible IL experiences, their school librarians were most likely required to compete with the curriculum that teachers were charged with delivering. Based on our experiences with preservice teachers and graduate students who are studying to become school librarians, this is still the case.

Many schoolteachers view their time with their students as limited when they review the instruction that must occur for learning and to prepare students for testing. When this happens, school librarians must advocate for what they can do to help teachers and students. If they advocate for teaching IL knowledge and skills, school librarians might find they have more time to help students grow in their IL ability while supporting classroom teachers in the teaching they need to do. If school librarians can approach IL through different subject areas, such as English/Language Arts and science or history, then they can begin to develop the ability in students to transfer their IL knowledge and skills between the subject areas. The goal should be for the school librarian to purposefully plan how this will occur. Selecting a specific inquiry method to use with the entire school, such as Guided Inquiry[23] brings all subjects and levels together in how students inquire, curate, and engage with information. Outcomes should be identified and assessed. Planning, execution, and assessment of IL knowledge and skills will help the school librarian identify areas for improvement and advancement. Ideally, school librarians should use the AASL National School Library Standards and the accompanying frameworks to achieve transferability of IL knowledge and skills to new subject matter and environments, such as when students enter college.

Within the AASL Standards, there are six Shared Foundations that include (1) inquire, (2) curate, and (3) explore. The three listed here are also part of ACRL's Framework for Information Literacy for Higher Education, which includes research as inquiry, searching as strategic exploration, and information creation as a process. There is commonality between the two sets of standards and foundations. As an individual grows from Pre-K–12 schooling into the university environment, IL knowledge should be built upon every year.

A place that is easy to begin is with young children who are still inquisitive about their surrounding world. Their questions can have answers that require more information for them to grow. This is an opportunity that should not be missed. As they grow older, their questions will become more focused and include their learning and personal interests. Following their interests will keep learners engaged as they curate information. School librarians can build upon the foundation laid when students were younger and can continue to support their growth in IL knowledge and skills. Purposefully teaching IL knowledge and skills will help students become lifelong learners who navigate the vast amount of information they will face at university and in their daily lives.

CONCLUSION

School librarians play a crucial role in preparing students for college success. They offer guidance and guardrails in student information-seeking, helping to create habits that will support their endeavors in college and beyond. One of the lesser-acknowledged aspects of information-seeking is that it is not only contextual but also developmental in nature. Student understanding of how to meet their own information needs is built upon all their learning experiences regarding information-seeking strategies throughout their school careers. Guided inquiry, the process of searching with support, provides the best and most facile way for students to learn information-seeking skills. It teaches techniques and acknowledges the emotions that occur throughout the information-seeking process. It is the use of AASL standards as a lead-up to the ACRL framework for higher education that will ensure students obtain and maintain the skills and abilities to find what they seek throughout life.

NOTES

1. Patricia Iannuzzi, et al., "Information Literacy Competency Standards for Higher Education" (Chicago: American Library Association, 2000), 5.
2. Rae-Anne Diehm and Mandy Lupton, "Learning Information Literacy," *Information Research*, 19, no. 1 (2014): 3.
3. Iannuzzi et al., "Information Literacy Competency Standards for Higher Education," 8.
4. Constance Mellon, "Library Anxiety: A Grounded Theory and Its Development," *College & Research Libraries*, 47, no. 2 (1986): 160–165.
5. Elizabeth McAfee, "Shame: The Emotional Basis of Library Anxiety," *College & Research Libraries*, 79, no. 2 (2018): 237–256.
6. Qun Jiao, Anthony Onwuegbuzie, and Art Lichtenstein, "Library Anxiety: Characteristics of 'At-Risk' College Students," *Library & Information Science Research*, 18, no. 2 (1996): 151–163.
7. Onwuegbuzie and Jiao, "The Relationship Between Library Anxiety and Learning Styles Among Graduate Students: Implications for Library Instruction," *Library & Information Science Research*, 20, no. 3 (1998): 235–249.
8. Onwuegbuzie and Jiao, "I'll Go to the Library Later: The Relationship Between Academic Procrastination and Library Anxiety," *College & Research Libraries*, 61, no. 1 (2000): 45–54.
9. Onwuegbuzie and Jiao, "The Relationship Between Library Anxiety and Learning Styles Among Graduate Students: Implications for Library Instruction."
10. Onwuegbuzie and Jiao, "I'll Go to the Library Later: The Relationship Between Academic Procrastination and Library Anxiety."
11. Ibid.
12. Jacob Lackner, "Confronting Library Anxiety," *Public Services Quarterly*, 18, no. 3 (2022): 224–231.
13. Onwuegbuzie and Jiao, "I'll Go to the Library Later: The Relationship Between Academic Procrastination and Library Anxiety."
14. Zoe Blecher-Cohen, "The Student Connection: Thinking Critically on Library Anxiety and Information Literacy," *Journal of Information Literacy*, 12, no. 2 (2018): 4–23.
15. Melissa Gross and Don Latham, "Attaining Information Literacy: An Investigation of the Relationship Between Skill Level, Self-Estimates of Skill, and Library Anxiety," *Library & Information Science Research*, 29, no. 3 (2007): 332–353.
16. Blecher-Cohen, "The Student Connection: Thinking Critically on Library Anxiety and Information Literacy."
17. Sloan Komissarov and James Murray, "Factors That Influence Undergraduate Information-Seeking Behavior and Opportunities for Student Success," *The Journal of Academic Librarianship*, 42, no. 4 (2016): 423–429.
18. Blecher-Cohen, "The Student Connection: Thinking Critically on Library Anxiety and Information Literacy."

19. Miri Shonfeld, Noa Aharony, and Noa Nadel-Kritz, "Teachers' Perceived Information Literacy Self-Efficacy," *Journal of Librarianship and Information Science*, 54, no. 3 (2021): 1–14.

20. Shonfeld, Aharony, and Nadel-Kritz, "Teachers' Perceived Information Literacy Self-Efficacy."

21. Veronica Cunningham and Dorothy Williams, "The Seven Voices of Information Literacy (IL)," *Journal of Information Literacy*, 12, no. 2 (2018): 4–23, http://dx.doi .org/10.11645/12.2.2332.

22. Rachel Ranschaert, "Authority and Carnival: Preservice Teachers' Media Literacy Education in a Time of Truth Decay," *Educational Studies*, 56, no. 5 (2020): 519–536.

23. Carol Kuhlthau, Leslie Maniotes, and Ann Caspari, *Guided Inquiry Design: A Framework for Inquiry in Your School* (Santa Barbara, CA: Libraries Unlimited, 2012).

13

Information Literacy in High Schools

DESIGNER LIBRARIANS NEEDED

Brenda Boyer, Lecturer, School of Communication and Information,
Rutgers University, New Jersey

The instructional role of high school librarians has always been important for learner success. Librarians not only open and expand the world of literature and resources for students, but also teach young adults how to be savvy in the overwhelming world of information. In an era of rampant misinformation, over-reliance on devices, and quick consumption of headlines rather than a deeper understanding of news, this role is crucial.

Research has strongly reinforced the importance of librarians and library programs for student learning.[1] Information literacy (IL) skills, in particular, are essential to college readiness.[2] Teaching these skills requires a strategic approach, one that requires librarians to step into the role of instructional designers. The concept of "designer librarian" refers to the requisite need for school librarians to be full instructional partners and leaders in instructional design in their schools. Understanding the full scope of a school's curriculum is the first step. From their unique vantage point, librarians can see opportunities for integrating high-quality resources into the existing curriculum as well as spots where IL skills are not only needed but could enhance the value and relevance of the classroom instruction they accompany. American Association of School Librarians (AASL) Standards provide a framework for instructional goals for K–12 librarians. A review of the wider curriculum reveals instructional goals to be targeted by educators. Together, these two sets of standards present powerful collaborative opportunities for teaching IL skills.[3]

Having identified opportunities for teaching IL skills, the next and perhaps most critical step is determining which skills are needed and how these skills should be taught. Information literacy skills are widely defined and include skills that fall into three broad categories: information management, critical thinking, and metacognitive reflection. Information management skills are often the chief focus of high school librarian instruction: the "how-to" nuts and bolts instruction necessary to get students locating resources, logging in to databases, performing searches, managing references, and citing sources. In a study exploring the research skills of college first-year students, information management skills were consistently those in which the students expressed the highest confidence levels and identified as having learned in high school.[4] In many schools, especially those lacking librarians or having wide student-to-librarian ratios, these foundational skills may represent the lion's share of what is possible. While information management skills are obviously important, they become truly powerful tools when paired with critical thinking.

Research is a thinking process. Critical thinking IL skills represent the "why" of research: why it is important to brainstorm keywords, evaluate sources for credibility, recognize bias, and summarize and integrate ideas learned from sources. Here, learners consider if statistics provided in sources are truly significant. They seek additional viewpoints for balance, form effective searches, and formulate research questions and thesis statements. These tactics evidence learners' grasp of the strategies needed for successful research projects because they demonstrate that the learner understands why they are performing different tasks (as opposed to simply doing "steps" of research). Critical thinking skills can be modeled by librarians as they are teaching information management skills. Providing the "why" of each step and demonstrating how decisions are made at each juncture in the process push learners to become more intentional in the decisions inherent in the research process. In many ways, being able to engage in the thinking processes of research is a dividing line between successful and unsuccessful student research products. For example, high school-age learners are often more focused on getting a project done, rather than enjoying the learning journey. They are looking to be finished with their projects as quickly as possible. This disposition often leads to a focus on creating the final product of their inquiry (writing the paper, making the movie, slides, etc.) before they have constructed new knowledge (i.e., learned anything new). Of course, the problem here is that if they have not engaged with their research resources in a meaningful way, there really isn't anything to present. Reminding learners that research is an iterative thinking process, the results of which are expressed in writing (or film, or presentations, etc.) helps maintain a focus on the learning happening during the process. Metacognitive thinking takes the learning one step further.

Metacognitive skills "evoke a higher understanding of the overall research process and may affect not only the outcome of a research project but also whether the learning occurring in a research experience is transferable."[5] Metacognition, commonly referred to as "thinking about thinking," is widely recognized as important to learning and the transfer of skills from one learning event to the next. Metacognitive learners reflect on their research process, what is working, what is not working, and what other paths might be taken. It is knowing how and where to seek assistance. It is recognizing when different or additional information is needed to answer a research question. It is visualizing the connections between and across research findings. It is also being able to reflect on the entire research process, their own IL skills, and the success of their inquiry product. Although it is critical to have learners perform some metacognitive reflection at the close of a project, this type of deep reflection needs to occur during the process, where it can most affect learning outcomes.

Information management steps, critical thinking skills, and metacognitive reflection need to be presented, practiced, and learned simultaneously for the skills to stick, improve, and transfer to subsequent learning events. Occasional "one-shot" approaches, pathfinders, and resource lists fall short in the face of growing demands for deeper IL skills in our schools. Librarians must incorporate these resources and strategies into the development of comprehensive and targeted approaches to their teaching. Armed with an understanding of curricular goals of subject area teachers and the need to teach IL skills concurrently, high school librarians can collaborate with colleagues to develop impactful instructional designs. In addition to collaboration, successful instructional designs in secondary schools hinge upon digital tool integration and differentiation.

While school librarians have traditionally been early adopters of digital tools and many have found their roles morphed to include technology coaching for colleagues, sometimes the "why" of tool usage was (and sometimes still is) tenuous. Librarians need to be ready to suggest ways that tools and apps can be optimized and combined to facilitate learning and creation during the inquiry process. Differentiation demands that the needs of individual learners be recognized and met. Targeted integration of digital tools makes this level of differentiation and personalization possible. Learning management systems and interactive video tools provide excellent frameworks for differentiation as they provide varied assessment tools and learning pathways that scaffold students as they move toward learning targets. Scaffolding high school learners through differentiated paths also increases the relevance of library-related skills when they are introduced, presented, practiced, and learned via collaborative teacher-librarian partnerships.

Inquiry models such as Guided Inquiry[6] and the Stripling Model[7] provide research-proven frameworks for collaborative research projects. Each of these models provides ample critical thinking and metacognitive reflection for learners as they work through an inquiry project. Correctly implemented, each model slows down the research process to make it explicitly intentional (i.e., learners think about their processes, successes, and failures, and adapt as they go). Of course, many short-term opportunities occur throughout the school year where the collaboration might be limited to a single day. Sometimes, the only option for librarians is to take a "quick start" approach to teaching specific IL skills (e.g., doing single sessions on topics like recognizing bias, information evaluation, and citing sources). Even these brief encounters can be enriched by incorporating and stressing points of critical thinking about decisions inherent in the skill and explicitly modeling and eliciting learner reflection on the skill performance to increase the odds of transfer of the skill. For librarians, the instruction cannot end at the close of that single lesson. Follow-up sessions for learners who are struggling need to be incorporated into the librarian/teacher plans, along with ongoing individual support continually offered in the library for all IL skills.

The importance of personal relevance for what librarians are teaching to individual learners cannot be overstated. Young adults need to see that what their teachers want them to learn actually matters in their lives. Subject area teachers and librarians need to build elements of personal choice into instructional designs for high school learners. Offering choice in the topics they will apply their IL skills toward, as well as the nature of their products of inquiry, demonstrates respect and empathy for students. Incorporating hands-on options (e.g., using the makerspace for building prototypes or research products) or authentic applications of skills to community issues or projects reinforces that IL/research skills aren't just for school; they are valuable in real life.

Combining learning targets (i.e., curriculum goals) with IL skills taught in the context of authentic inquiry that reinforces choice and honors differentiation is a winning combination for instructional design success. Go on, be a designer librarian!

NOTES

1. Keith Curry Lance and Debra Kachel, "Why School Librarians Matter: What Years of Research Tell Us," *Kappan*, 99, no. 7 (April 2018): 15–20.
2. Brenda Boyer and Ewa Dziedzic-Elliott, "What I Had, What I Needed: First-Year Students Reflect on How their High School Experience Prepared Them for College Research," *Journal of Academic Librarianship*, 49, no. 4 (July 2023): 102742.
3. American Association of School Librarians (AASL). National School Library Standards for Learners, School Librarians, and School Libraries (ALA Editions, 2018).
4. Brenda Boyer and Ewa Dziedzic-Elliott, "What I Had, What I Needed: First-Year Students Reflect on How their High School Experience Prepared Them for College Research," *Journal of Academic Librarianship*, 49, no. 4 (July 2023): 102742.
5. Brenda Boyer and Ewa Dziedzic-Elliott, "What I Had, What I Needed: First-Year Students Reflect on How their High School Experience Prepared Them for College Research," *Journal of Academic Librarianship*, 49, no. 4 (July 2023): 102742.
6. Carol Collier Kuhlthau, Leslie Maniotes, and Ann Caspari, *Guided Inquiry: Learning in the 21st Century* (Exeter: Libraries Unlimited, 2015).
7. Barbara K. Stripling, "Inquiry-Based Learning," in *Curriculum Connections through the Library* (Exeter: Libraries Unlimited, 2003).

14

Media Literacy and High School Students

Olga Polites, Adjunct Professor of Composition, Rowan University, New Jersey

In the twenty-first century, media literacy is more important than ever. Constantly changing and new technologies require us to keep up with and update our critical thinking skills in order to be well-informed, healthy, responsible citizens.

When I started teaching English in the early 1980s, students used virtually no digital resources when completing their academic work. Going to the library meant learning how to use a card catalog and microfiche, a flat piece of film containing micro-photographs that was fed into a reader with a screen. Printed paper copies of newspapers, magazines, and journals were stacked on long shelves that seemed to go on forever. Since editors and experts vetted all library materials, students never had to worry about the credibility of the sources they were accessing.

Once the internet became available and resources began migrating to digital platforms, students and teachers had to learn a whole new way of conducting research. How to use databases, search engines, and Boolean logic all became necessary and important skills to learn.

As students became more comfortable using the World Wide Web, they began to use the internet for their research rather than the digital databases available to them. They most frequently cited the ease of typing a search query to get information rather than sifting through all the different database platforms that their libraries provided. The problem was that they needed to learn how to recognize whether information was true or false and know how to locate, evaluate, use, and communicate information in various formats.

Today, high school students' level of media engagement is constant. As they move closer to making lifelong decisions about school and career choices, the ability to critically think about the information they access will have profound effects on their future success. And it doesn't end with school-related activities; they will be making important decisions in their personal and civic lives as well.

NEWS MEDIA

One of the first industries to see the profound effects of our Digital Age is newspapers. Advertising, which was their number one source of revenue, disappeared as companies migrated to digital platforms. From 2005 to 2021, about 2,200 local print newspapers closed, creating news deserts in many parts of the country.[1] While many newspapers have online editions, it has been challenging to grow subscribers when so many online news sites give away their content for free.

SOCIAL MEDIA

Before Meta (formerly Facebook) became a global phenomenon, few could have imagined how one company could have such a profound effect on culture. What started as a platform for connecting people with similar interests has morphed into a company that shares news information, although there are no mechanisms in place to verify the credibility of these sources.

Today, students use YouTube, TikTok, Snapchat, and Instagram not only to entertain themselves but to access information about every aspect of their lives. According to Pew Research Center, "Roughly nine-in-ten teens say they use YouTube. . . . Majorities of teens ages 13 to 17 say they use TikTok (63%), Snapchat (60%) and Instagram (59%)."[2]

These are astounding numbers, and research shows that as each class of students graduates from high school, more of them rely specifically on TikTok as a news source.

ARTIFICIAL INTELLIGENCE

We no longer ask questions about just how much digital media affects our daily lives. With artificial intelligence, the latest technology to date, we must ask, "Is what I'm seeing real, or not?" This is why it's so important that students learn how the technology revolution affects every part of contemporary life.

A PLAN OF ACTION

Teaching media literacy to high school students need not be a complicated process. Whether it's in a ninth-grade social studies class or a twelfth-grade English class, students should learn:

Olga Polites

- the basics of rhetoric and argument
- how algorithms work
- how to fact-check claims and sources.

We need to teach media literacy within a digital framework. Media is almost always a for-profit structure; therefore, students need to learn how that profit structure works, and that they are, in fact, the product. They are not just content creators, but also distributors of content. By learning these concepts in all classes, students will better understand how much the digital world impacts their lives.

THE BASICS OF RHETORIC AND ARGUMENT

Rhetorical Situation

An effective way to start looking at written and visual texts is to determine the rhetorical situation; this involves identifying such things as the speaker, audience, subject, occasion, purpose, and tone.

- The **speaker**, or rhetorician, may be an orator, writer, cartoonist, advertiser, artist, photographer, documentarian, etc.
- The **audience** is the listener, reader, observer, and so on.
- The **subject** is the topic or issue being discussed and in what context.
- The **occasion** identifies the time and place the text was created, and why (exigency).
- The **purpose** is the goal that the rhetorician is trying to achieve.
- The **tone** is generally conveyed through the word choice the rhetorician uses to suggest an attitude. Tone can be described as playful, serious, sarcastic, formal, informal, etc.[3]

Rhetorical Choices

After identifying the rhetorical situation, it's time to examine the various ways in which a rhetorician appeals to his or her audience. The most common are ethos, pathos, and logos.

Appeals to ethos are based on the character, credibility, or reliability of the writer. These types of appeals are a way to build trust, as well as emphasize shared values between the speaker and the audience.

Pathos is an appeal to emotions, values, and hopes, as well as fears and prejudices. While considered a weak strategy to build an argument, it can be employed very effectively.

Appeals to logos rely on logic or reason. There is a clear main idea, specific details and examples, facts, statistics, research, expert testimony, etc.

In addition to appeals, rhetoricians make stylistic choices regarding language when crafting their argument. For example, they may use repetition or imagery in order to bring about a particular effect on the audience. Here are a few examples:

- figurative language (simile, metaphor, extended metaphor, personification, symbol)
- repetition, anaphora
- rhetorical questions
- irony, sarcasm, paradox
- satire
- hyperbole, understatement[4]

A good example to use in teaching these concepts is Martin Luther King Jr.'s "I Have a Dream" speech, delivered at the Million Man March in Washington, DC, on August 28, 1963. First, students will determine the rhetorical situation:

- Speaker: MLK, leading civil rights activist, well-educated, minister
- Audience: directly: Black marchers, civil rights activists, government leaders; indirectly: President Kennedy, TV audience
- Occasion and Subject: Million Man March, Washington, DC, 1963, a peaceful demonstration regarding civil rights
- Purpose: to inspire his audience to promote changes necessary to abolish discrimination
- Tone: concerned and serious but hopeful; motivational, passionate

Then, students will determine the appeals and the style choices the speaker employs:

- Ethos: *personal experience; minister; appeals to our sense of justice; unifying language—"our hope," "our freedom"*
- Pathos: *metaphors* (manacles, chains); *extended metaphor* (the check); *allusions* ("valley of despair"); *children*
- Logos: *Emancipation Proclamation, Declaration of Independence, church bombing*

Learning the basics of rhetoric is the first step to developing arguments. Students must first be able to identify the elements in other writers' arguments before they can write their own.

Argument

Argument is finding, through a process of rational inquiry, the best solution to a complex problem or issue. As we engage with the issue, we try to suspend judgment and delay closure by engaging thoughtfully with alternative points of view, truly listening to other perspectives, examining our own values and assumptions, and perhaps even changing our views. There are no winners and losers in this type of academic argument; instead, we have a much better understanding of the issue, with a goal toward problem-solving.[5]

Defining features of argument:

- requires justification of its claims
- is both a process and a product
- combines truth-seeking with persuasion.

Basic elements of argument:

- thesis: writer's position/opinion on an issue
- reasons: claims used to build an argument
- evidence: supports the line of reasoning

As students become more familiar with the basics of rhetoric and argument, they will more critically analyze the information they engage with.

HOW ALGORITHMS WORK

An algorithm is a set of commands that must be followed for a computer to perform calculations or other problem-solving tasks. This may sound clinical and neutral, but algorithms reflect the biases of the computer programmer. Students need to learn how algorithms work in order to understand how the content they consume on their digital devices is customized based on their previous search queries.

Algorithms are a foundational building block of our digital world—they often shape our experiences online in more ways than we realize. On a given day, we might encounter an algorithm that recommends what video we should watch on YouTube, one that filters our search results on Google, and another that determines whether other people see our comment on TikTok.[6]

Here are three videos that explain how algorithms work:

- Using Google: https://www.youtube.com/watch?v=pu_Ox3HcfKc[7]
- Algorithmic Bias Explained: https://www.youtube.com/watch?v=tia5OHE98F4[8]
- How YouTube's Algorithms Can Fool You: https://www.youtube.com/watch?v=CuFKYSSZtpo[9]

After watching these videos, students will have a much better understanding of how algorithms directly affect the content they consume on their social media sites and why they need to verify the credibility of that information.

FACT-CHECKING CLAIMS AND SOURCES

One way to help students determine the credibility of the information they are accessing is to teach them how to be quick fact-checkers. Mike Caulfield, a research scientist who specializes in social networks and online information literacy at the University of Washington, created the SIFT method for verifying claims and sources: Stop; Investigate the Source; Find Better Coverage; Trace Claims. This allows students to quickly see whether or not they should engage more deeply with whatever media they have accessed.

In these short videos, students can learn how to become good fact-checkers:

- How to Find Better Information Online: Click Restraint: https://www.youtube.com/watch?v=gbPEiCGxVVY[10]
- Online Verification Skills—Video 1: Introductory Video: https://www.youtube.com/watch?v=yBU2sDlUbp8&t=34s[11]
- Online Verification Skills—Video 2: Investigate the Source: https://www.youtube.com/watch?v=hB6qjIxKltA&t=28s[12]

In addition, Caulfield wrote *Web Literacy for Student Fact Checkers*: https://pressbooks.pub/webliteracy/front-matter/web-strategies-for-student-fact-checkers/[13]

Teaching digital media literacy skills need not be a complicated, time-consuming task. Since high school students engage in a wide variety of subjects, it's important for teachers to tailor their lessons around their areas of expertise. Digital technology will continue to dominate our lives, so the more opportunities students get to develop their media literacy skills, the better they will be able to discern credible, reliable information. They will then build knowledge and competencies in using media and technology, and be better prepared in making decisions regarding their health, careers, and civic lives.

NOTES

1. Joiner, Whitney, and Alexa McMahon, "Since 2005, about 2,200 Local Newspapers across America Have Closed. Here Are Some of the Stories in Danger of Being Lost — as Told by Local Journalists," *The Washington Post Magazine*, November 30, 2021, https://www.washingtonpost.com/magazine/interactive/2021/local-news-deserts-expanding/.
2. Anderson, Monica, Michelle Faverio, and Jeffrey Gottfried, "Teens, Social Media and Technology," Pew Research Center, December 11, 2023, https://www.pewresearch.org/internet/2023/12/11/teens-social-media-and-technology-2023/.
3. Bean, John, June Johnson, and John Ramage, *Writing Arguments: A Rhetoric with Readings*. New York: Pearson Longman, 2011, 32.
4. Ibid.
5. Ibid.

6. Henderson-Hood, Erikk, and Daniel Vargas Campos, "Do Algorithms Influence Our Lives and Our Democracy?" *Common Sense Education*, June 24, 2022, https://www.commonsense.org/education/articles/do-algorithms-influence-our-lives-and-our-democracy.

7. Kansas University Libraries, "Using Google," YouTube Video, https://www.youtube.com/watch?v=pu_Ox3HcfKc.

8. Institute for Public Policy Research, "Algorithmic Bias Explained," YouTube Video, https://www.youtube.com/watch?v=tia5OHE98F4.

9. Above the Noise, "How YouTube's Algorithms Can Fool You," YouTube Video, https://www.youtube.com/watch?v=CuFKYSSZtpo.

10. Digital Inquiry Group, "How to Find Better Information Online," YouTube Video, https://www.youtube.com/watch?v=gbPEiCGxVVY.

11. CTRL-F. "Online Verification Skills—Video 1: Introductory Video," YouTube Video, https://www.youtube.com/watch?.

12. CTRL-F, "Online Verification Skills—Video 2: Investigate the Source," YouTube Video, https://www.youtube.com/watch?v=hB6qjlxKltA&t=28s.

13. Caulfield, Michael *Web Literacy for Student Fact-Checkers* (Pressbooks, 2017), https://pressbooks.pub/webliteracy/front-matter/web-strategies-for-student-fact-checkers/.

15

Teaching Students to Decode the World

LIBRARIANS AS LEADERS FOR MEDIA LITERACY

Chris Sperry, Director of Curriculum and Staff Development, Project Look Sharp, New York

In 1996, when Project Look Sharp (PLS) first started working with educators to integrate media analysis into their teaching, we encountered a consistent refrain: "I don't have the time to add one more thing to my curriculum." In the decades since, that refrain has only grown stronger. But those same teachers also said: "I can do it if I can use media literacy to teach my core content and engage more students." Since that time, PLS has been developing the resources, training, and support that enable all educators to integrate curriculum-driven media analysis throughout the Pre-K–12 curriculum.

PLS is a not-for-profit initiative based at Ithaca College. It has pioneered the classroom methodology of Constructivist Media Decoding (CMD)[1] where educators use student-centered, question-based media analysis to integrate habits of critical thinking into the core curriculum. The PLS website, www.projectlooksharp.org, includes over 850 free standards-aligned lessons that use engaging media documents (from books to blogs and songs to social media) to teach content area knowledge and skills with critical thinking about media messages. The website includes many free resources about the CMD process as well as videos, slide sets, and presenter guides for providing professional development about CMD.[2] Over the last three years, PLS has collaborated with school librarians and school library systems, first in New York state and now nationally, to scale up this work.

This chapter will describe why this approach is essential, what it looks like in the classroom, why and how librarians can be the leaders in bringing this to both their students and colleagues, and the resources available for implementing this approach in all schools.

MEDIA ANALYSIS ACROSS THE CURRICULUM

The last decade has taught us that our democracy is dependent upon a media-literate citizenry, armed with the habits of critical thinking and personal reflection that will give them, as Thomas Jefferson said, sufficient education to enable them to exercise oversight. But how do we give *all* students both the empowerment that comes when we diversify the media forms focused on in school, and the orientations needed for continual scrutiny of media messages?

PLS's approach, CMD, assumes that each student constructs their own understanding of the world based on their lived experience and identity. Good teaching requires that we listen well to our students' meaning-making and facilitate learning in the classroom that maximizes their openness to progressively more complex understandings of the world. Traditional modes of teaching emphasize the acquisition of specific knowledge that students can repeat back on standardized tests. Today's infodemic of conflicting and often fraudulent ideas requires that we teach students from Pre-K through high school graduation to perpetually analyze, evaluate, and create media in diverse ways. See model of figure 15.1: *Process of Media Literacy Graphic* below.

We develop habits when we continually practice something. We would not conceive of teaching students to read solely through a ninth-grade class or a series of library lessons. The same is true for learning to read media messages. A singular media literacy lesson, or even a full media literacy course, no matter how terrific, is unlikely to develop habits of critical thinking about

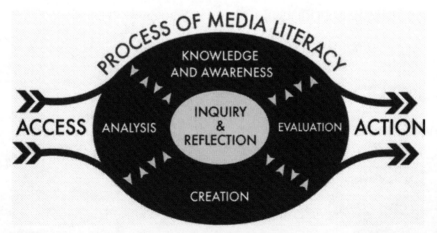

Figure 15.1 Process of Media Literacy Graphic. *Source*: Project Look Sharp.

all media messages. But when we integrate habits of thinking at all levels and into diverse subjects—with continual practice in varied contexts that evolve in complexity—we will educate a more reflective, discerning, and empowered citizenry.

"I DON'T HAVE THE TIME!"

Asking teachers to add anything new to their already overburdened curriculum is a tough sell. But we *can* show all teachers how engaging students in media analysis that has them learn and apply core subject area knowledge can be a more effective way of teaching to our standards without taking more time. With the correct media documents and questions (see *Categories and Sample Questions for Media Decoding* below), and with skilled facilitation linked to one's objectives but based on student meaning-making, media decoding lessons can effectively address the "I don't have the time" concern. In the process, it can enfranchise all students in learning.

MEDIA ARE MASS-PRODUCED MESSAGES THAT USE TECHNOLOGY TO COMMUNICATE ACROSS TIME AND SPACE.

This includes social media, websites, AI, games, films, photographs, newspapers, books, paintings, songs, charts, maps, money, advertising, and a host of other forms, including some yet to be created.

All teachers use media in the classroom, including textbooks, posters, charts, and graphs. Like all media, these are made to educate, persuade, and/or entertain. Educators regularly use video clips and websites to inform students about subject area content. AI will be progressively used in schools for multiple purposes. These media messages are created and promoted by individuals, organizations, corporations, or governments for particular purposes, typically for a target audience. While all educators use media in their teaching, even if only books, they have the ability (and responsibility) to repurpose those messages for critical thinking as well. (See figure 15.2.)

All media are created by sources that have points of view or biases, even if the bias is to present "both sides." They use a particular language of construction that is tied to their media form. They have contexts that shape their meaning. They have diverse impacts on individuals and on society more generally. And media messages are interpreted differently by different people.[3] Whenever we use media in the classroom, we should consider asking at least one question that has students reflect on the constructed nature of that media message and/or their own interpretation. By repurposing media in the

CATEGORIES AND SAMPLE QUESTIONS FOR MEDIA DECODING
DEVELOPING HABITS OF INQUIRY AND REFLECTION

AUTHORSHIP & PURPOSES

- Who made this and for what purposes?
- What do they want me to do, think or feel?
- Who is the target audience?

ECONOMICS

- Who paid for this?
- Who might make money from this and how?

CONTENT

- What are the messages about _____?
- What values, ideas and biases are overt or implied?
- What is left out that might be important to know?
- Whose voices are included and whose are left out?
- How does this compare to other messages on this topic?

TECHNIQUES

- What techniques are used to communicate the messages?
- Why might they have chosen to use those techniques?
- Was this crafted to trigger emotions, if so, how and why?

CONTEXT

- When was this created and how was it shared?
- What aspects of historical or cultural context are relevant to consider?
- How does this reinforce or counter cultural norms?
- How does the technology or media form (social media, print, TV, etc.) impact the message?

CREDIBILITY

- Is this fact, opinion, or something else (fiction, satire, etc.)?
- What are the sources of the ideas or assertions?
- How do I know this is believable or accurate?
- Is this a trustworthy source about this particular topic?
- How might I confirm this information using reliable sources?

EFFECTS

- How does this make me feel and why?
- What impact might this have on others or on society?
- Who might this message benefit? Who might it harm?

INTERPRETATIONS

- How and why might different people interpret this differently?
- How do my experiences and identity shape my interpretation?
- Do I have an open mind on this? Why or why not?
- What do I learn about myself from my interpretation or reaction?

RESPONSES

- What questions do I have about this?
- What knowledge do I need to fully understand this? How do I find that information?
- Will I share this? If so, how and with whom? If not, why not?
- What kinds of actions might I take in response to this?

FOLLOW UP WITH...

- What is my evidence?
- Why do I think that?
- How could I find that out?
- Why might this matter?

Figure 15.2 Categories and Sample Questions for Media Decoding. *Source*: Cyndy Scheibe, Chris Sperry, and Faith Rogow.

classroom to include media literacy questions, we can infuse habits of critical thinking about media messages across the curriculum.

"Now I'm like a woodpecker, asking: Why do you think that is? Where do you think that's leading?"[4]

ML3 Librarian

MEDIA DECODING VS. MEDIA LITERACY

It is important to clarify that teaching students to habitually question media messages, while an essential component of literacy in the twenty-first century, does NOT give students ALL the skills and knowledge needed to be media-literate. Students also need to be creators of their own media and, in the process, reflect on their decision-making about their own messages.[5] In addition, students need core information about the role of media in society, the techniques of communication in various forms (e.g., artificial intelligence literacy), and explicit instruction in cyber safety, news literacy, etc. Many excellent resources are available for teaching these media literacy skills and knowledge.[6] The CMD approach advocated here will give students continual practice in asking good questions about all media messages and in reflecting on their own meaning-making. This approach gives *all* educators an effective and accessible methodology for using media in any classroom that not only teaches these habits and core subject area content, but also gives educators a practice for student-centered, inquiry-based teaching.

"This has completely changed how I approach my job. . . I've realized how many of my questions were accidentally very biased. So, using a constructive media decoding approach even to information questioning changed how students were responding, and it was better. More open-ended questions; more student-centered."

ML3 Librarian

In a traditional classroom, the educator presents information, often through a lecture or media document (text, video, website, etc.), and expects students to "learn the content." CMD repurposes mediated information from content to be memorized for critical thinking and reflection. CMD shifts our conception of teaching from filling students up with information to teaching students to apply what they know, analyze and evaluate sources, assess what they need to know, and reflect on their own thinking.

"Almost 3/4 of ML3's school librarians made a profound shift in their teaching practice, from teacher-centered information delivery to student-centered inquiry. This change influenced everything they taught, not just CMD."

Faith Rogow from the ML3 Evaluation

This shift in pedagogy is necessitated by the revolutionary changes in our information ecology. When I began teaching in the 1970s, giving students access to information was still a primary focus. Today, our students are overwhelmed with limitless information—some of it misleading, if not outright false. The shift from giving students information to teaching them to apply, analyze, evaluate, and reflect on information still holds knowledge as essential in learning, but it centers our teaching on our students rather than on the content.

CONSTRUCTIVIST MEDIA DECODING IN PRACTICE

In the words of media literacy scholar Faith Rogow, "Constructivist Media Decoding takes general concepts like inquiry and discussion and analysis, and it makes them real in a concrete way on the ground."[7] The best way to get a picture of CMD in action is to watch it in the classroom. On PLS's homepage, there is the button "Demonstrations of Media Decoding," where you will find over twenty short, annotated videos showing CMD at different levels and for diverse subjects. In all these models, the teacher has clear subject area objectives, including teaching knowledge and concepts. They have chosen one or more engaging media documents and crafted initial questions that target those goals. And they facilitate the decoding by selectively probing student responses. (See figure 15.3.)

One can witness the art of CMD in the way an educator responds to student interpretations of media documents. While students provide the analysis, the teacher leads the discussion through their choice of how and when to probe, guiding students toward learning objectives. Traditionally, when a student gives the "correct" response to a question, the teacher moves on. In CMD, the teacher uses that student to teach their peers by a response such as, "Tell me more about that." To have students learn evidence-based analysis, the teacher might ask, "Where do you see that in the document?" To assess the group's view of a particular interpretation, the teacher can tell the class, "Raise your hand if you agree." To have students assess strategies for answering their own questions, the teacher can ask, "How could we find that out?" or to have students ask their own questions, "What questions do you have about ____?"

Figure 15.3 Screen grab of demonstration video. *Source*: Project Look Sharp.

Chris Sperry

And occasionally, a teacher may need to respond directly to a potentially hurtful comment by saying, "I need to challenge that."

CMD is based on the recognition that each student constructs their own understanding. As much as we wish we could fill students up with knowledge, that is not how learning works. CMD is a literacy process that teaches students to, in the words of Brazilian educator Paulo Freire, "read their world."[8] It is an inquiry process focused on questions—by the teacher and ultimately by the students. It incorporates subject area knowledge into the analysis of diverse media documents. It has students reflect on their own thinking, including their own biases for confirming what they already believe.

METACOGNITION, MEDIA, AND BIAS

We know that confirmation bias is a powerful force in shaping what we believe and what we reject. Just telling students "the facts" is no longer enough to protect the truth, if it ever was. Research by Kahne and Bowyer has shown that media literacy initiatives that have high school students reflect on their own biases are essential in teaching them to effectively distinguish truth claims in the media.[9] We teach this essential practice when we ask students questions like, "Why might some people think differently than others about this?" "How does your experience or identity impact how you evaluate the credibility of this source?" Or with our youngest students, "What feelings does this bring up for you?" and "Why might that be?"

In the 1960s and 1970s, networks like ABC, NBC, and CBS, that vied for the largest swath of American eyeballs by catering to the middle of the political spectrum, dominated the media landscape. Views at the margins did not fit into Walter Cronkite's closing catchphrase to the daily news, "And that's the way it is." Beginning with talk radio in the 1980s, then cable news, the internet, and social media, we now have an information ecosystem that filters us into echo chambers that reinforce our existing beliefs. This profound shift in how we receive information needs to be met with a pedagogical shift in how we approach mediated information in our schools.

"We want our students to internalize this [CMD inquiry] strategy. Yeah, it's a habit. It's a strategy of being able to think critically and ask questions. And you know, it's something that kind of transcends... being able to demonstrate that we can have civil discourse and disagree and still be able to get along. I feel like that could go a long way into resolving some of the polarization that's taken root in our country and caused such deep divides."

ML3 Librarian

Challenging polarized thinking through civil conversations and metacognition; teaching students to evaluate credibility and bias through evidence-based questioning; preparing students to deal with mis-, dis-, and mal-information; reaching traditionally disenfranchised and marginalized students; enhancing student engagement and agency; and training educators to listen to student meaning-making are some of the benefits of CMD. But how can we scale up this work in all schools for all students?

ML3: LIBRARIANS AS LEADERS OF MEDIA LITERACY

CMD needs an advocate in every school who can model this methodology with students and also share resources and provide professional development for their colleagues. School librarians are the information literacy specialists in our schools. They are experienced with inquiry and experts in collaboration. They often know all students, map all curricular areas, and have connections to all teachers. They are positioned to be instructional leaders and have a commitment to protect truth and safeguard well-reasoned thinking about mediated messages. School librarians are the logical leaders of this work.

In 2021, PLS received a two-year grant from the Booth Ferris Foundation in partnership with the New York State School Library Systems Association. The "Librarians as Leaders for Media Literacy in New York Public Schools" (ML3) Initiative aimed to scale up the work of PLS to enable the integration of critical thinking and media literacy in schools across New York state through the leadership of K–12 public school librarians.[10] The pilot worked intensively with nineteen Pre-K–12 librarians, library system directors, and coordinators across all regions of the state. Over the two years, the ML3 librarians and the New York State School Library System directors identified the resources, training, and support needed for scaling this work across the state.

By winter 2023, ML3 had done full-day professional development workshops with over 1,500 New York librarians, facilitated yearlong follow-up groups in dozens of regions, and collaborated with PLS in the creation of new ML3 materials, such as:

- Dozens of **media decoding lessons** coauthored by school librarians for integrating CMD into the Pre-K-12 library curriculum, including:
  - *How Do I Choose? Picking the Right Book for Me*—by Sharon Fox
  - *Discovering Ramadan*—by Michele Coolbeth
  - *Columbus "Discovers" America: What's The Story?*—by Roma Matott
  - *TikTok Timebombs: Methods of Media Manipulation*—by Beth Cuddy
  - *Censoring Seuss: Cancel Culture or Cultural Respect?*—by Susan Allen
  - *Global Perspectives Through Movie Posters*—by Arlene Laverde[11]
- A new **Librarian Created Materials** page that includes an online game, bulletin boards, flyers, and other resources.

Chris Sperry

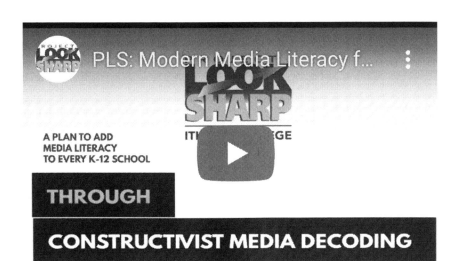

Figure 15.4 Screen grab ML3—CMD video. *Source:* Project Look Sharp.

- Short **videos that explain CMD,** including **a nine-minute video** overview of ML3.
- Resources for **delivering professional development** in schools about CMD including *Handouts, Tips for Collaboration* and *Advocating,* and *Videos* to use in delivering professional development, as well as *Slide Sets* and *Presenter Guides* for delivering professional development for different amounts of time to different professional audiences.
- A hybrid **self-paced course** that teaches librarians to deliver CMD to students. Librarians are also using this course to teach their teachers CMD by combining the asynchronous modules with face-to-face leading of practice decodings.

"I learned just how much better my teaching can be by participating in ML3 and I wish that this could be a part of every teacher training program and mandated in every state—it would change the face of education, and likely shift the fractious thinking in our country if implemented." ML3 Librarian

SCALING UP ML3

In August 2023, the federal Institute of Museum and Library Services awarded a two-year grant to PLS in partnership with the American Association of School Librarians, and in collaboration with the National Association for Media Literacy Education (NAMLE), to plan how to scale this work nationally. ML3 aims to not only bring habits of critical thinking about all media messages to all students, but to reform education through repurposing the use of media in the classroom via an accessible method and materials for student-centered, inquiry-based teaching. This approach will help empower all students to have a stronger voice in their learning, to develop the skills of citizenship and orientations of democratic engagement, and to address the human need to read and write our worlds.

For more information about the ML3 initiative, go to www.projectlooksharp.org.

NOTES

1. See a five-minute video about CMD at www.projectlooksharp.org.
2. See https://www.projectlooksharp.org/?action=PD_resources.
3. See https://namle.net/.
4. All ML3 Librarian quotes available in the *ML3 Evaluation Report*: bit.ly/43PJ2YV.
5. See *Questions ... for Media Creation*: projectlooksharp.org.
6. See https://namle.net/.
7. From the video: *Constructivist Media Decoding* at projectlooksharp.org.
8. Freire, P. (1970). *Pedagogy of the Oppressed.* New York: Herder and Herder.
9. Kahne, J., and Bowyer, B. (2017). "Educating for Democracy in a Partisan Age: Confronting the Challenges of Motivated Reasoning and Misinformation," *American Educational Research Journal, 54*(1), 3–34.
10. See projectlooksharp.org.
11. Search Project Look Sharp lessons by *Keyword* (e.g., "disinformation"), *Subject* (e.g., Library/Information Literacy), *Age/Grade level*, and filter your search by *Media Type* (e.g., Social Media), *Duration* (e.g., Under 15 min.), *Standards*, etc.

16

Student Inquiry Moves

CUSTOMIZING PERFORMANCE EVALUATION FOR SCHOOL LIBRARIANS

Deborah Lang Froggatt, Outreach Director, Massachusetts School Library Association, Massachusetts, and
Mary H. Moen, Associate Professor of Library and Information Studies, University of Rhode Island, Rhode Island

How does it look when a librarian is facilitating information literacy in the context of inquiry research, library use, reading, and confident, critical thinking? What should an evaluator observe during performance evaluations when students are engaged in learning behaviors in the library? In the United States, school librarians (SL) are often evaluated using the general classroom teacher performance rubric. The established process frequently yields little cognizance of SL's evidence-based practices, pedagogies, and effective learning impacts.[1,2,3] Subsequently, SLs are challenged when facing their annual performance evaluations because content-specific expertise in information literacy is often omitted from teacher rubrics used by their evaluators.[4,5,6] Information literacy is the ability to recognize when information is needed and to "locate, evaluate, and use effectively the needed information"[7]—key skills that SLs teach that are critical across all content areas for student success.

When administrators use generic classroom rubrics, they may describe classroom learning activities, but the majority are without SL performance evaluation specificity. This denies evaluators strategies for gauging SL effectiveness, including inquiry learning, information literacy instruction, and collaborative leadership.[8,9] Misconceptions of the SL's value may ultimately lead to program or SL reductions.[10] Thus, equitable access to high-quality library programs and pedagogies that SLs offer may be compromised, denying students opportunities to acquire lifelong inquiry skills required for participating in our global community.[11]

The International Federation of Library Associations and Institutions' School Library Guidelines note that "school librarians are rarely evaluated in a consistent and systematic way."[12] One way to customize performance evaluation instruments for SLs is to include student look-fors, a term that describes observable student behaviors and actions. Student look-fors provide detail about what students do when learning. The more detailed and content-specific the scoring rubric is, the more consistent and reliable teacher performance evaluations will be,[13] and it is easier to provide specific feedback to teachers to help them develop professionally.[14] Thus, providing distinct and explicit examples, such as student look-fors in an observation instrument for SLs, can increase the quality, fairness, and usefulness of evaluations.

The adoption of student look-fors introduces a shared language that aligns with the American Association of School Librarians' (AASL's) recommendation to use student-centered growth measurements in SLs evaluations. SL should be "evaluated with instruments that address their unique responsibilities and contributions according to established district practices for all professional personnel."[15] While the term "student look-fors"[16] may not be explicitly utilized within the SL profession, the student-centered nature of inquiry learning inherently encompasses observable student behaviors, information literacy action, and dispositions, aligning seamlessly with the concept of student look-fors.

To delve into SL-specific evaluation rubrics, we examined which states had SL-specific performance evaluation rubrics. A total of seventeen (33.3 percent of all states) were found, sixteen from individual states and one from the District of Columbia. These were primarily developed by state education departments or school library associations. Subsequently, an examination of whether these rubrics include "student look-fors"[17] was undertaken, aimed at identifying observable student behaviors within library learning environments. As we explored the rubrics with "student look-fors,"[18] four discrete themes emerged. To conceptualize these themes under one term, we deem them as *student inquiry move look-fors* (SIM), the unique, observable behavior of students as they learn in the library.

Table 16.1 illustrates an example of an SL performance evaluation rubric with SIM look-fors. The first column describes the categories being evaluated; the second, third, and fourth columns describe highly effective, competent, and developing competency levels. The fifth column provides examples of evidence that evaluators may observe, and the SIM look-fors we identified are in bold.

The analysis of SL performance evaluation rubrics revealed four distinct types of student behaviors or SIM look-fors—Inquiry Researchers, Library Users, Accomplished Learners, and Readers—each reflecting specific aspects of student engagement within the library environment. Together, these paint a picture of students as observable inquiry learners in the library.

Table 16.1 Example of SL-Specific Rubric Elements

Category	Highly Effective	Effective	Developing	Evidence
Knowledge of Content and Instructional Planning				
Inquiry Based Learning - A program where **students are challenged to question, think critically acquire, evaluate, draw conclusions, and create and share new knowledge which answers a research question.**	Librarian has developed and is consistently implementing and promoting a collaboratively planned inquiry-based program which challenges students to research, reflect, synthesize, and produce knowledge products.	Librarian has developed and is often promoting a collaboratively planned inquiry-based program which challenges students to research, reflect, synthesize, and produce knowledge products.	Librarian is developing and has started planning collaboratively an inquiry-based program which challenges students to research, reflect, synthesize, and produce knowledge products.	Research driven by essential question - SL acts as a research guide - Written teaching goals, objectives, with timelines - **Students create knowledge products, often with the use of technology** - Evidence of student statistics, data, and analysis
Instructional Practice: Teaching for Learning				
Information Literacy and Technology - Librarian teaches information and literacy skills and the use of technology for learning.	Librarian consistently promotes information literacy skills throughout the building and consistently plans instruction based upon a written curriculum. Librarian consistently recommends technology tools to enhance instruction and is a building leader modeling tech tools and information literacy principles.	Librarian often promotes information literacy skills throughout the building and often plans instruction based upon a written curriculum. Librarian often recommends technology tools to enhance instruction.	Librarian sometimes promotes information literacy skills at some grade levels and is developing a curriculum.	**Student projects display use of multiple valid information sources** - **Students' knowledge products often involve media creation and/ or other technology integration** - **Students successfully navigate information and misinformation** - **Students can articulate the need to cite sources.**

Figure 16.1 represents the conceptual framework of students as inquiry learners and the four types of observable behavior and their sub-categories that emerged from the analysis of school librarian performance evaluation rubrics. The four sub-categories that emerged under the Inquiry Researcher category were Explorer, Curator, Creator, and Evaluator, which align closely with the AASL Shared Foundations. The Library User typology highlights student engagement with technology and active participation in library programs. This mirrors the increasing integration of technology in education, reaffirming the crucial role of librarians as technology leaders. The Accomplished Learner category showcases behaviors related to time management, responsible conduct, and higher-level thinking skills, all essential for holistic student development and success. The Reader category emphasizes students' abilities to navigate and share diverse genres independently, inherently tied to information literacy—a skill crucial for lifelong learning.

Table 16.2 below provides examples of SIM look-fors from the rubrics we analyzed for each of the Inquiry Researcher sub-categories: Explorer, Curator, Creator, and Evaluator. These observable behaviors are core information literacy skills.

Table 16.3 provides examples of *SIM look-fors* from the SL performance evaluation rubrics we analyzed for the Library User sub-categories of technology, space/programs, and resources/services. Information technology has changed the way students learn, and the fact that technological tools are ubiquitous,[19,20] suggests that SL should be viewed as technology leaders, confirming the expertise that the profession wields. How students use the library space

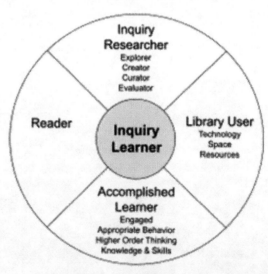

Figure 16.1   Inquiry Learner SIMS Conceptual Framework. *Source*: Mary Moen.

Deborah Lang Froggatt and Mary H. Moen

Table 16.2 SIM Look-fors for the Inquiry Researcher sub-categories

Inquiry Researcher	Explorer	Curator	Creator	Evaluator
Examples of SIMs from SL Performance Evaluation Rubrics	explore a variety of ideas independently seek print, digital materials	ethically use information share new knowledge	create products that demonstrate new learning creates essential questions (from Common Core State Standards), curriculum inquiry projects (from performance indicators)	uses rubric for assessing own research skills students self-assess their work

Table 16.3 Examples of *SIM Look-fors* for the Library User Sub-category

Library User	Technology	Space/Programs	Resources/ Services
	use visual, digital, textual, and technological formats independently interact with technology to enrich and extend research	engaged in a gaming club; after school program use library for a variety of activities function independently in the library	use digital resources (all students, special needs, ELLs, gifted) use mobile netbooks, e-readers, and tablet computers browse and borrow from the technology collection

and resources are indicators that "the school library is a unique and essential part of a learning community."[21]

Table 16.4 provides examples of *SIM look-fors* for each of the sub-categories in the Accomplished Learner category. These examples support Lance's suggestion that SLs are essential in helping students develop the dispositions and high-level thinking skills for success, "the crux of what we now call 21st century skills."[22]

Table 16.5 shows examples of *SIM look-fors* for the Reader category. Reading is a skill inherent in information literacy and academic success.

Table 16.4 Example of *SIM Look-fors* in the Accomplished Learner sub-categories

Accomplished Learner	Engaged	Appropriate Behavior	Higher Order Thinking	Knowledge and Skills
	self monitor their work and behaviors of others	assumes considerable responsibility for the smooth operation of routines and procedures	use varied representations to engage thinking, support understanding, develop skill acquisition	use technology for engagement in higher-level content & skill development
	with the SLT, establishes rules for learning & behavior	use routines and procedures to develop appropriate behavior	use strategies for independent, creative & critical thinking	use information literacy models.

Table 16.5 Examples of *SIM Look-fors* in the Reader category

Reader				
	engage with appropriate information resources building on interests	leisure reading activities

Reading for pleasure and personal growth | electronic auto-summarizing tool in word processing programs to aid reading comprehension | appropriate independent reading materials |

Deborah Lang Froggatt and Mary H. Moen

These examples of SIM look-fors provide evaluators and SLs with language that describes students as inquiry learners. Thus, these concepts can be used to develop an evaluation rubric specifically for SLs.

Operationalizing SIMS within a performance evaluation rubric takes planning and collaboration. Here is a success story: A team of Boston Public Schools librarians worked with the human capital department to adapt and adopt the non-compulsory Massachusetts Department of Education and the Massachusetts School Library Association School Librarian Performance Evaluation Rubric.[23] The Boston Public Schools (BPS) Interactive Rubric served as a guide and embellished the state's classroom teacher evaluation regulations by adding "Student Look-fors."[24] After engaging in action research that showed demonstrable student learning for their performance evaluations and observations, the BPS Librarians developed content-specific school library/information literacy look-fors.[25] Now, BPS evaluators can use the BPS School Library Student Look-fors rubric when evaluating an SL[26] and engage in an "ongoing dialog"[27] about the impact that SLs have on student learning and acquiring information literacy skills.

Incorporating student look-fors, such as those described in the SIM's Inquiry Learner Framework, in performance evaluations can be a win-win for SLs and school leaders. This comprehensive and flexible model, rooted in AASL Standards and information literacy skills, provides a robust framework for evaluating the effectiveness of SL. Utilize this tool to engage in constructive dialogues with evaluators, ultimately enhancing professional practice and the evaluation process.

NOTES

1. Lance, Keith. "The Mind of a Researcher," *Teacher Librarian,* 37, no. 4 (2010): 82.
2. Lance, Marcia Rodney and Bill Schwarz. "The Impact of School Libraries on Academic Achievement: A Research Study Based on Responses from Administrators in Idaho," *School Library Monthly,* 26, no. 9 (2010): 14–17. https://eric.ed.gov/?id=EJ886979.
3. Library Research Service, "School Libraries Impact Studies." https://www.lrs.org/school-libraries/impact-studies/.
4. Hartzell, Gary. "The Principal's Perceptions of School Libraries and Teacher-Librarians," *School Libraries Worldwide,* 8, no. 1 (2002): 92–110. https://doi.org/10.29173/slw7102.
5. Haycock, Ken. "Evaluation: The Person or the Program?," *Teacher Librarian,* 27, no. 2 (1999): 14–23. https://eric.ed.gov/?id=EJ603700.
6. Pon, Terrance. "Evaluation of the Teacher-Librarian: Review of the Models," *School Libraries in Canada,* 24, no. 3 (2005): 37–43. http://journal.canadianschoollibraries.ca/wp-content/uploads/2017/04/SLiCv24n3.pdf.
7. American Library Association. "Evaluating Information: Information Literacy." Last modified June 27, 2022. https://libguides.ala.org/InformationEvaluation

/Infolit#:~:text=From%20the%20ALA%20Presidential%20Committee,use%20
effectively%20the%20needed%20 information.

8. American Association of School Librarians (AASL). *National School Library Standards for Learners, School Librarians and School Libraries* (Chicago, IL: ALA Editions, 2017).

9. Kuhlthau, C. C., Maniotes, L. K., and Caspari, A. K. *Guided Inquiry: Learning in the 21st Century*. Westport, CT: Libraries Unlimited, 2015.

10. Lance and Briana Francis. "The Impact of Library Media Specialists on Students and How It Is Valued By Administrators and Teachers: Findings from the Latest Studies in Colorado and Idaho," *Tech Trends*, 58, no. 4 (2011): 63–69. http://dx.doi.org/10.1007/s11528-011-0513-9.

11. Froggatt, Deborah Lang. "Making It Real: Growing Inquiry Learning Instructors," In *Global Action for School Libraries: Models of Inquiry*. Edited by Barbara Schultz-Jones and Dianne Oberg. Berlin and Boston, MA: De Gruyter Saur, 2022, 215–225.

12. International Federation of Library Associations and Institutions School Libraries Section Standing Committee. "IFLA School Library Guidelines," Second Revised Edition. International Federation of Library Associations, 2015, 46. https://www.ifla.org/wp-content/uploads/2019/05/assets/school-libraries-resource-centers/publictions/ifla-school-library-guidelines.pdf.

13. Johnson, Evelyn, Yuzhu Zheng, Angela Crawford, and Laura Moylan. "Developing an Explicit Instruction Special Education Teacher Observation Rubric," *The Journal of Special Education*, 53, no. 1 (2019): 28–40. https://doi.org/10.1177/0022466918796224.

14. Hill, Heather and Pam Grossman. "Learning from Teacher Observations: Challenges and Opportunities Posed By New Teacher Evaluation Systems," *Harvard Educational Review*, 83 (2013): 371–384. https://doi.org/10.17763/haer.83.2.d11511403715u376.

15. American Association of School Librarians (AASL). *National School Library Standards for Learners, School Librarians, and School Libraries* (ALA Editions, 2018), 175.

16. "Interactive Rubric Overview." Boston Public Schools Office of Human Capital.

17. Boston Public Schools Office of Human Capital.

18. Boston Public Schools Office of Human Capital.

19. Johnston, Melissa. "School Librarians as Technology Integration Leaders: Enablers and Barriers to Leadership Enactment," *School Library Research*, 15 (2012): 1–33. https://www.ala.org/aasl/sites/ala.org.aasl/files/content/aaslpubsandjournals/slr/vol15/SLR_School_Librarians_as_Technology_Integration_Leaders_V15.pdf.

20. Kuhlthau, Maniotes, and Caspari. *Guided inquiry: Learning in the 21st Century* (Westport, Conn: Libraries Unlimited, 2015).

21. American Association of School Librarians (AASL). *National School Library Standards for Learners, School Librarians, and School Libraries* (ALA Editions, 2018), 11.

22. The Mind of a Researcher: Keith Curry Lance.(FROM THE BRAIN TRUST). Teacher Librarian (Vancouver). Vol. 37. Bowie: E L Kurdyla Publishing LLC, 2010.

23. "Rubrics." Massachusetts Department of Elementary and Secondary Education, accessed December 3, 2023, http://www.doe.mass.edu/edeval/rubrics/.

24. "Interactive Rubric Overview." Boston Public Schools Office of Human Capital, accessed, October 31, 2023, https://www.bostonpublicschools.org/Page/416.

25. Froggatt. "Making It Real: Growing Inquiry Learning Instructors." In *Global Action for School Libraries: Models of Inquiry*. Edited by Barbara Schultz-Jones and Dianne Oberg. Berlin and Boston, MA: De Gruyter Saur, 2022, 215–225.

26. "Implementation Support for School Librarians." Boston Public Schools Library Services, accessed October 25, 2018, https://www.bostonpublicschools.org/libraryservices.

27. American Association of School Librarians (AASL). *National School Library Standards for Learners, School Librarians and School Libraries* (ALA Editions 2018), 155.

17

Academic and School Library Partnerships Focused on Professional Development in Information Literacy

Neil Grimes, Education and Curriculum Materials Librarian,
William Paterson University, New Jersey; and
Gary Marks Jr., Reference and Outreach Librarian, William Paterson
University, New Jersey

Before school librarians can provide teachers and districts with guidance on implementing information literacy (IL) into their instruction, they need to become IL experts, be trained in IL, and be fluent in instructional strategies. This professional development (PD) training can occur from an individual school-university partnership, as is presented later in the chapter as a case study between William Paterson University and the school librarians and other educators in New Jersey's Paterson Public Schools or as a result of a statewide partnership between librarian organizations. A recent partnership between the New Jersey Association of School Librarians (NJASL), the College and University Section of the New Jersey Library Association, and the NJ Chapter of the Association of College & Research Libraries (NJLA-CUS/ACRL-NJ) resulted in college and career readiness sessions and subject-specific research introductions for high school students to help alleviate feelings of library anxiety as they make the transition from secondary school to their college and university studies.[1] The partnership also led to an organization-led approach to PD and the development of a statewide community of practice for the instruction of IL for K–16 education in New Jersey.

Professional development is essential in education as it provides K–12 educators, including school librarians, with the skills to teach in an ever-changing world. Through the course of this chapter, the authors seek to define PD, discuss traditional vs. online PD, provide background on school libraries/librarians and the need for IL PD for school librarians, discuss academic library partnerships with K–12 schools, present a case study of a 1:1 school-university partnership focused on online PD, offer insights into a recently formed state-wide library organizational partnership and its plans for online PD for school librarians, and conclude with the implications of local and statewide partnerships involving academic and school librarians focused on PD.

All educators, including K–12 school librarians, must be lifelong learners to teach future generations of students. In the twenty-first century, K–12 education is in an era of school reform and constant change. "Many school leaders see the potential for PD as the key to educational improvement."[2] PD, whether in person or online, presents the opportunity for improvement in teaching and learning. It can lead to transformative change in school culture within K–12 organizations. It can be provided in-house with educators in a school organization, such as school librarians leading PD for school faculty, or through school-university partnerships or other established partnerships. It can even emerge from unexpected places, such as a school-university partnership with an academic library or through academic librarians. In response to the COVID-19 pandemic, many schools shifted PD for their K–12 faculty, including school librarians, to the online environment.

It is the authors' perspective that the goal of PD is progressive instructional improvement due to the teacher training provided at a school or district level. Through PD provided by academic librarians, school librarians, and other K–12 educators can become more fluent in IL, more familiar with current digital learning tools, and even be introduced to the latest emerging technologies like augmented reality, virtual reality, and artificial intelligence.

DEFINING PROFESSIONAL DEVELOPMENT AND A NEW STRATEGIC ROLE FOR ACADEMIC LIBRARIES

"Professional development is defined as activities that develop an individual's skills, knowledge, expertise and other characteristics as a teacher."[3] The development of teachers beyond their initial training will help build a more vital teaching force. PD can update individuals' subject content knowledge and pedagogical techniques. Teachers can apply current educational research to their professional practice through this ongoing training. Effective PD allows for an exchange of information and expertise among teachers, teacher trainers, and academic scholars. This results in changes to a school organization's curricula and teaching practices, as well as an improvement in educational outcomes for students and overall teacher retention rates.[4]

Traditional forms of PD have been face-to-face "pull-out" programs to implement new curricula or pedagogies.[5] This PD model does not have a lasting impact on school climate as it is considered to be a "just in time" approach.[6] Additionally, traditional approaches to PD fail to provide ongoing professional mentoring for entry-level teachers. This lack of support is a significant factor underlying the nearly 50 percent attrition rate among K–12 teachers during their first five years in the classroom.[7]

There are an estimated 116,867 libraries of various kinds in the United States, with 3,094 being academic libraries.[8] Although the number of academic libraries is small compared to public and school libraries, academic libraries exist in every U.S. state and geographic region in the United States. With the rise of online meeting platforms such as Skype, Zoom, Cisco WebEx, and Google Meet, academic libraries and librarians can connect online with some of the 90,400 public and private K–12 schools across America.[9] The example of a school-university partnership presented in this chapter focuses on a new strategic direction for academic libraries involving a partnership with K–12 schools to provide PD on a district-wide or single-school basis to enhance the skillsets of school librarians and other K–12 educators. Through a school-university partnership, academic librarians can support K–12 educators in IL, educational technologies, and literacy instruction for teaching and learning at the 90,400 K–12 public and private schools across America.[10]

ONLINE PROFESSIONAL DEVELOPMENT IN THE PATERSON PUBLIC SCHOOLS—A CASE STUDY

When COVID-19 curtailed traditional K–12 education in the Paterson Public Schools, the David and Lorraine Cheng Library (William Paterson University) offered support to K–12 teachers, including school librarians, by providing online PD. The first online session was offered at the beginning of September 2020, just before the K–12 school year started. The authors co-taught the session using Google Meet and conducted it for three and a half hours. Attendees included thirty-eight K–12 technology teachers and fourteen K–12 school librarians. The title of the first online PD session was *Creating and Supporting Research Projects During Remote Instruction—A Collaborative Process*. Resources to support online teaching and learning and specific resources to support project-based learning activities were shared using a Google document outline and made accessible through a publicly available LibGuide developed and managed by the authors.[11] The outline of the PD session (Google document) and the LibGuide were shared with all participating educators during the session and via email after the session.

Before conducting the first online PD session, the authors met for an hour and collaborated using a Google document to frame an outline of their presentation. During the weeks leading up to the session, the authors populated the outline by curating specific resources to share with the K–12 technology teachers and K–12 librarians. Overall, the first online PD proved successful, as

Table 17.1 XXXXX

Table 1: PD Session Ratings.

(N = 29)	Excellent	Good	Needs Improvement
Q. Effective activities that promote learning	14 (48%)	14 (48%)	1 (>2%)
Q. Overall, how would you evaluate this professional development session	12 (41%)	16 (55%)	1 (>2%)

evidenced by the positive feedback from a post-PD session survey. Out of the fifty-two educators who attended, twenty-nine answered the feedback survey. Of the respondents, twenty-three indicated that they would recommend the PD training to teachers in their building, and twenty-eight respondents rated the PD training as "Good" or "Excellent" (table 17.1). Respondents provided qualitative feedback in the post-training survey to aid in developing future PD training sessions. This feedback included comments about the application of the session's content, the timing for preparation to begin the school year, and requests for follow-up sessions with more advanced content (table 17.2).

The following online PD session supported eighty-six middle school and high school social studies teachers in the Paterson Public Schools, highlighting resources to support students' historical research as part of the National History Day competition. This session was an hour-long program hosted via Google Meet. This online PD session was titled *National History Day 2020—Workshop, Resources, and Support.* While this session focused on subject-specific educators, the value of the online PD session led to additional PD opportunities within the district. Following the online PD session, fifty-eight social studies teachers completed the post-PD survey. The overall evaluation of the PD session indicated thirty-one thought it was Excellent, seventeen believed it was Good, and ten deemed it as Fair. An open-ended question was posed to all PD participants: "In what ways will this training enhance your skills in your current position?" Common trends gathered from the participants' responses included supporting students competing in the New Jersey National History Day competition, developing more project-based learning (PBL) activities, and developing lesson plans incorporating history and research.

Following the success of the first two district-wide online PD sessions, the principal of International High School (IHS), one of the twelve high schools in the Paterson Public Schools,[12] contacted one of the authors inquiring about additional PD for her school. IHS is an International Baccalaureate (IB) School. The IB program is a rigorous college preparatory program where students must complete multiple research-based assignments. The author assisted with student research projects by conducting two one-hour online PD sessions for forty

Table 17.2 XXXXX

Table 2: *Qualitative Responses Q. Please feel free to provide additional feedback about today's session Please feel free to provide additional feedback about today's session*

R1. "Good information and will implement for future lessons."

R2. "I like the thematic planning/research. Websites and platforms that support remote learning and promote collaborative project outcomes are what we need. So much time is spent on searching for these vehicles hopefully this will help."

R3. "I felt this workshop was very interesting, now I just need to play with the tools, web sites, and applications mentioned in this training so that I can confirm my level of mastery of the content. I believe a follow-up training would be useful after a month for teachers to have more informed questions."

R4. "I would like to see a more advanced follow-up to this!"

R5. "During the first days of school, Technology teachers have to create over 15 classes, input over 400 students in their Google Classrooms, think about planning introductory lessons for the first days of remote teaching, etc. It was great information but would serve us better later in the year. I think we all need more lessons on the Google platform since many of us have more experience in the Microsoft platform. For example, we need more PD on how to organize our Google Drive, How to effectively use Go Guardian with students, How to organize and effectively use our Google mail, best practices being used in K-8 technology classes, etc. I think that the Librarians and high school teachers got more out of this PD than the K-8 Technology teachers. The timing was off, but great information! Thank you☺"

high school faculty members on *Project-Based Learning (PBL) and Research across the Curriculum.* The first session was held in early November 2020 and focused on defining PBL, how to collaborate with the school librarian on lesson planning, and teaching specific IL skills. The IL skills highlighted included forming a research question, conducting research using databases, evaluating sources, using a research note sheet as students read and analyze their sources, forming an outline, and transitioning from an outline to focused writing.

The second session for the faculty of IHS was held in November 2020 and focused on continuing the first online PD session. This session began with a review of the previous session, highlighting specific resources that would encourage teachers to develop PBL activities that immersed the students in the learning process and how to incorporate online learning tools, conduct PBL activities, and do research related to subject content areas. Additional resources were shared from a Library Research Guide that one of the authors created, highlighting online teaching and learning resources[13] as well as resources from the NJASL in a wakelet.[14]

During this second online PD session, one of the authors was able to share resources and best practices on how to teach about racism, injustice, structural inequality, and issues of equity through PBL activities using resources he curated in the area of culturally responsive education (CRE) in a Library Research Guide.[15] A NJASL wakelet on the issues of equity, diversity, and inclusion, which presented innovative ways for educators to teach students and involve students in PBL activities, provided additional resources for IHS educators.[16]

Beyond the focus on PBL and CRE resources, one of the authors shared the work of Sophia Joffe, who was a twelfth-grade student back in 2020 from Toronto, Canada. She created eLearn.fyi, a database of more than 300 online learning tools for teachers and students in response to the COVID-19 pandemic.[17] Additionally, the author shared a free e-book with the faculty at IHS that highlighted stories of educators across the United States and their innovative ways of providing instruction to students during the COVID-19 pandemic. The e-book was titled *Teaching, Technology, and Teacher Education during the COVID-19 Pandemic: Stories from the Field.*[18]

Overall, the PD sessions successfully introduced curated high-quality resources to the faculty of IHS that focused on research across the curriculum, PBL, online resources for teaching and learning, and resources that addressed culturally responsive teaching for a K–12 student population. In an hour-long online PD session with an academic librarian, educators were provided with a variety of online resources to assist them with lesson planning, encourage PBL activities, help them engage in culturally responsive teaching, and create innovative learning experiences for their students using the many curated collections of resources.

After the two single-school PD sessions were rated as successful, a central administrator in the Paterson Public Schools contacted one of the authors to provide two more district-wide online PD sessions. These sessions would focus on training all school librarians and technology teachers at one online PD session and all social studies teachers at another session on how to use the Smithsonian Learning Lab, a free, interactive platform for discovery, creation, and sharing.[19] The Smithsonian Learning Lab is a collaborative teaching and learning tool allowing authentic learning and PBL experiences.

Through his online PD sessions, one of the authors provided an overview of the Smithsonian Learning Lab, information on registering for an account, searching for and exploring resources, starting a collection, and adding resources into a collection using a PowerPoint presentation. One of the authors shared two thematic collections and two lesson-specific teaching collections at the two online PD sessions. He had collaboratively built these collections while working with two professors-in-residence (PIRs) who are a part of the professional development schools (PDS) network at William Paterson University. The author's involvement with the Smithsonian Learning Lab developed because of a grant given by the Smithsonian Institution to the College of Education. The grant allowed the author to work with PIRs in building the two thematic[20,21] and two teaching collections[22,23] to be used in two schools in the Paterson Public Schools that are a part of the 60-plus schools that make up the PDS network of schools in northern New Jersey.[24,25]

It is the authors' perspective that preparing K–12 students to engage in PBL activities that teach students elements of the research process and help students to develop IL skills prepares them for the different types of PBL activities they will complete at the college or university level. To support school librarians, other K–12 teachers, and their students, the authors advocate for PD focused explicitly on the PBL approach. This approach incorporates IL and helps students develop research, note-taking, critical thinking, and often writing skills.

Powers and de Waters state that "teaching with project-based learning requires students to tackle a problem. The PBL approach is consistent with national and state standards and has been shown to improve the understanding of basic concepts, to encourage deep and creative learning, and to develop teamwork and communication skills."[26] In preparing K–12 students for careers in the twenty-first century, school administrators and leaders should consider incorporating the PBL approach throughout their school's curricula. The common thread woven into PBL instruction is the educators' choice to turn over most of the learning to their students. PBL calls for a shift from teacher-led instruction to student-driven learning experiences with support from librarians and content-specific educators throughout the PBL process.

NEW JERSEY STATEWIDE LIBRARY ORGANIZATIONS FORM PARTNERSHIP

While establishing the organizational partnership between NJASL and NJLA-CUS/ACRL-NJ, a survey was developed and disseminated in 2022 to ascertain the wants and needs of New Jersey school librarians. This survey sought feedback from school librarians regarding the college and career readiness panels offered to high school students and where school librarians saw opportunities to explore new avenues for expanding the organizational partnership. Sixty-three librarians responded to the survey. Respondents covered the spectrum of K–12 grade levels with ten (16 percent) Elementary Librarians, nine (14 percent) Middle School Librarians, thirty-two (51 percent) High School Librarians, two (3 percent) identified as K–12 Librarians, seven (11 percent) identified as both Middle School and High School Librarians, and three (5 percent) identified as Elementary and Middle School Librarians. See figure 17.1. Respondents selected from various options to rank the types of partnership activities they were most interested in seeing. The results appear in figure 17.2.

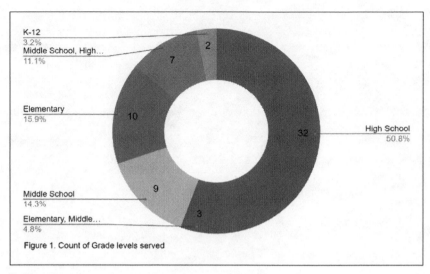

Figure 1. Count of Grade levels served

Figure 17.1 Count of Grade levels served. *Source*: Neil Grimes and Gary Marks

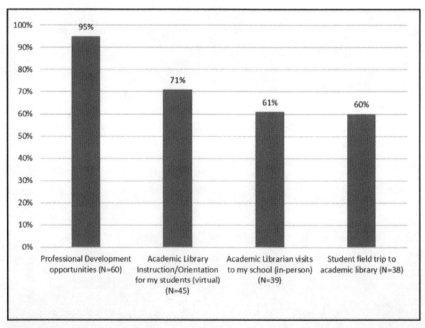

Figure 17.2 What Kind of Partnership Opportunities Are You Interested in? *Source*: Neil Grimes and Gary Marks.

As figure 17.2 demonstrates, K–12 librarians (95 percent) overwhelmingly favor PD opportunities (N = 60, 95 percent) as a priority in the new organizational partnership between school and academic librarians. The survey data led to a new pilot program where academic librarians provide online PD for New Jersey school librarians to strengthen their IL instruction. The new venture begins in February 2024 through an online teaching circle program named "Teaching Thursdays." During the online PD sessions, academic librarians serve as informal mentors by sharing lesson plans, teaching tools or resources, subject or course guides, or other instructional design tips and recommendations. The overarching goal is to develop a K–16 IL "community of practice" inclusive of K–12 school and academic librarians.

IMPLICATIONS OF LOCAL AND STATEWIDE PARTNERSHIPS FOCUSED ON PD

Successful partnerships can be created locally, as seen through the university-school partnership case study example between the Paterson Public Schools and William Paterson University. Based on the positive feedback received from the four district-wide and two single-school online PD sessions, online PD sessions to support K–12 school librarians and teachers will be the preferred approach for training and supporting educators on the local level moving forward. William Paterson University and the David & Lorraine Cheng Library plan to continue supporting the teachers and students of the Paterson Public Schools through online PD and library outreach efforts to support local schools. Although there is currently a limited number of partnerships between K–12 schools and academic libraries across the United States, the school-university partnership between the Cheng Library and the Paterson Public Schools has yielded positive results. Moving forward, academic library administrators and school district administrators hold the promise and potential to form new partnership with an academic library in their region, community, or state to provide library support through online PD sessions focused on IL, educational technologies, and other relevant topics. Beyond PD, these partnerships can provide additional in-person/online library instructional support toward integrating IL and PBL activities embedded in the K–12 curriculum. This partnership will help develop current and future teachers, including school librarians, and enhance learning for K–12 students across America.

Also, successful partnerships can be formed on the state level between professional organizations, as shown through a partnership between two statewide New Jersey library organizations presented in this chapter. PD provided through a statewide partnership between library organizations can benefit both organizations by supporting the PD of school librarians and other educators and meeting student learning outcomes, primarily focused on IL. Through an ongoing statewide organizational partnership between academic and school library organizations, academic librarians are piloting a new program to provide online PD for New Jersey school librarians to strengthen their IL instruction starting in early 2024. During the planned online PD sessions, academic librarians will serve as informal mentors by sharing a lesson plan, a teaching tool, or a subject or course guide with school librarians to model professional librarian practice and enhance school librarians' understanding of effective IL instruction. The lessons learned from these experiences will help guide the professional practice of IL and library instruction of New Jersey school librarians. PD for school librarians emphasizing IL will be critically important now and into the future as New Jersey became the first state in the United States in 2023 to require K–12 instruction on IL under the implementation of the New Jersey Student Learning Standards.[27] Other states will follow in passing similar legislation in the future.

CONCLUSION

Academic librarians will continue to contribute to the successful outcomes of school librarians, teachers, and students as more school leaders look to develop school-university partnerships that benefits the students and faculty at their K–12 school and in their school districts. Through statewide partnerships between library organizations, academic librarians can also provide ongoing PD in IL, educational technologies, and other areas that foster expertise and innovation in K–12 schools. Successful outcomes that can result from district-wide, single-school, or statewide partnerships involving academic libraries and librarians include well-trained school librarians and teachers on integrating IL and educational technologies throughout the K–12 curriculum. Furthermore, these outcomes can lead to better-prepared students for higher education and their future careers.

NOTES

1. Gary Marks Jr., Grimes, N., & Lafazan, B. (2023). "Academic and School Library Partnerships: An Organization-Led Collaboration." In *Cases on Establishing Effective Collaborations in Academic Libraries* (pp. 46–67). IGI Global.
2. Chris Dede. *Online Professional Development for Teachers: Emerging Models and Methods.* Cambridge, MA: Harvard Education Press, 2006, p. 1.
3. Organization for Economic Cooperation and Development (OECD). "The Professional Development of Teachers." In *Creating Effective Teaching and Learning Environments: First Results from TALIS* (OECD Publishing 2009), p. 49.
4. Organization for Economic Cooperation and Development (OECD). "The Professional Development of Teachers." In *Creating Effective Teaching and Learning Environments*: First Results from TALIS (OECD Publishing 2009), p. 49.
5. Dede, *Online Professional Development for Teachers*, p. 1.
6. Dede, *Online Professional Development for Teachers*, p. 1.
7. Dede, *Online Professional Development for Teachers*, p. 1.

8. American Library Association. "Library Statistics and Figures: Number of Libraries in the United States." LibGuides. June 2020. https://libguides.ala.org/librarystatistics.

9. National Center for Education Statistics. "NCES Fast Facts." https://nces.ed.gov/fastfacts/dailyarchive.asp.

10. Ibid should be National Center for Education Statistics. "NCES Fast Facts." https://nces.ed.gov/ fastfacts/dailyarchive.asp.

11. Grimes and Marks. "Online Resources for Teaching and Learning," David & Lorraine Cheng Library, William Paterson University of New Jersey, last modified March 21, 2023, https://guides.wpunj.edu/onlineresourcesteaching.

12. Paterson Public Schools. *Promising Tomorrows: Annual Report July 2018 - September 2020* (Paterson, NJ: Paterson Public Schools, 2020), pp. 1–2.

13. Neil Grimes. "Online Resources for Teaching and Learning: Home." LibGuides. March 2020. https://guides.wpunj.edu/onlineresourcesteaching.

14. Kim Zito. "Tools and Resources for Remote Instruction Curated by The New Jersey Association of School Librarians." Wakelet, 2020. https://wakelet.com/wake/118169c2-0557-47af-bc6b-0ed4dda85ccb.

15. Grimes. "Professional Development Schools Network: CRE." LibGuides. January 2021. https://guides.wpunj.edu/PIR.

16. NJASL Equity, Diversity, and Inclusion Committee. "NJASL Equity, Diversity, and Inclusion Resources." Wakelet. 2020. https://wakelet.com/wake/uwAzGB96xH_8LHHfHSfLD.

17. "Bulletin Board: [SpecialSections]." *New York Times,* October 18, 2020, Late Edition (East Coast). https://ezproxy.wpunj.edu/login?url=https://www.proquest.com/newspapers/bulletin-board/docview/2451584143/se-2.

18. Richard Ferdig, Emily Baumgartner, Richard Hartshorne, Regina Kaplan-Rakowski, and Chrystalla Mouza, eds. *Teaching, Technology, and Teacher Education during the COVID-19 Pandemic: Stories from the Field.* Waynesville, NC: Association for the Advancement of Computing in Education, 2020.

19. Smithsonian Institution. "Smithsonian Learning Lab." 2024. https://learninglab.si.edu/.

20. Grimes. "Paterson Public Schools (Don Bosco)—Theme—Identity." Smithsonian Learning Lab, April 2, 2021. https://learninglab.si.edu/collections/paterson-public -schools-don-bosco-theme-identity/RdUTGQEnm1jYkea7.

21. Grimes. "Paterson Public Schools (School #21)—Theme—Social Justice." Smithsonian Learning Lab, November 13, 2020. https://learninglab.si.edu/collections/paterson-public-schools-school-21-theme-social-justice/6mgb2wVMP9WREdoj.

22. Grimes. "Paterson Public Schools (Don Bosco)—Theme—Cultural Identity— Teaching Collection." Smithsonian Learning Lab, December 21, 2020. https://learninglab.si.edu/collections/paterson-public-schools-don-bosco-theme-cultural -identity-teaching-collection/RuZ2w09mKoV51Yrk.

23. Grimes. "Paterson Public Schools (School #21)—Theme—Social Justice -Teaching Collection." Smithsonian Learning Lab, December 21, 2020. https://learninglab.si .edu/collections/paterson-public-schools-school-21-theme-social-justice-teaching-collection/DFBJSa1nGkePRH4C.

24. William Paterson University, Office of Professional Development & School Community Partnerships. "Professional Development & School Community Partnerships."

William Paterson University, 2020. https://www.wpunj.edu/coe/departments/professional-development-schoolcommunity-partnership/Index.html.
25. William Paterson University, College of Education. "College of Education: Teaching as a Profession Information Guide." 2020. https://www.wpunj.edu/coe/departments/cert/assets/UG%20Education%20Brochure%209_16HR%20(1)%20Printable%20Version%20for%20Print%20Services.pdf.
26. Susan Powers and Jan de Waters. "Creating Project-Based Learning Experiences for University-K-12 Partnerships." In *34th Annual Frontiers in Education* (Frontiers in Education 2004), p. F3D–19.
27. Official Site of the State of New Jersey, Office of the Governor. "Governor Murphy Signs Bipartisan Legislation Establishing First in the Nation K-12 Information Literacy Education." January 4, 2023. https://www.nj.gov/governor/news/news/562022/20230104b.shtml.

Neil Grimes and Gary Marks

Index

training, staff, 30–31
truncation, 43
21st Century Skills, 150

visual literacy, 85, 107–14
Vygotsky, Lev 13

website evaluation, 42

Youtube, 128

Zone of Proximal Development
(ZPD), 13

About the Editor

Ewa Dziedzic-Elliott serves as the subject librarian for all departments in the College of New Jersey School of Education. She has ten years of experience as a K–12 librarian, including work in both elementary and high school settings. She holds a master's degree in library and information science from Rutgers University and a master of arts in Polish Language and Literature and teaching thereof from Jan Kochanowski University, Poland, EU. She also holds New Jersey supervisor and principal certifications. Her research interests include diversity and equity in collection management and barriers to information, especially in the immigrant, multicultural, and bilingual communities, information literacy, and multicultural and cultural literacies. She has published in the *Journal of Academic Librarianship*, *Library Connections*, and *Political Librarian*. She serves on the board of the New Jersey Association of School Librarians and on the editorial board for *Political Librarian*.

About the Contributors

Robbie Barber is an electrical engineer from Georgia Tech who wandered into a school library. As a teacher-librarian, she works with high school students and teachers to find the best resources, use the technology available, and locate the perfect book. Dr. Barber teaches classes on using research databases and how to better search the internet. She researches the latest educational technology and creates professional presentations on recognizing fake news and other tech-infused ideas for the classroom and media center.

Brenda Boyer is an instructor of graduate Library and Information Science (LIS) students in the School of Communication and Information at Rutgers University. Dr. Boyer has a master of library science (MLS) degree from Villanova University and a PhD in Instructional Design from Capella University. Throughout her career, Dr. Boyer has focused on the instructional role of librarians. With over three decades of experience as a school librarian, she has developed a wide variety of gamified library and information fluency instruction for secondary learners. Her experiences as an instructional designer include authoring and developing numerous online courses in the field of library science and information literacy, along with online graduate and professional development courses for educators. Dr. B's research interests include instructional design, information literacy, and the high school-to-college transition. She has written articles published in *The Journal of Academic Librarianship*, *Teacher-Librarian*, *Knowledge Quest*, *School Library Journal*, *School Library Connection*, and *Internet@Schools*.

Cathy Collins has worked as a library media specialist for over twenty years at the K–12 level. She holds a PhD in education with a specialization in curriculum, leadership, teaching, and learning; and additional master''s degrees in education and library science. She has published her writing in various journals, including *Education Week*, *Library Media Connection*, *NEA Today*, and American Association of School Librarians' (AASL) *Knowledge Quest*, and is the author of *Teaching News Literacy in the Age of AI: A Cross Curricular Approach*, which will be published by the International Society of Technology in Education (ISTE) in Spring 2024. She is a Fulbright/Teachers for Global Classrooms Fellow and the recipient of an AASL Intellectual Freedom Award. She is a 2023

Massachusetts School Library Association (MSLA) "Virtual Influencer" and 2023 Service Award recipient and was named an MSLA "Super Librarian" and Innovator. She is a member of the ISTE + Association for Supervision and Curriculum Development Board of Directors and served on the MassCUE Board as Professional Development Chair from 2015 to 2019. She is passionate about STEM/STEAM, global education, and media literacy. In addition to having coordinated the Chinese Exchange Program at Sharon High School for many years, she has journeyed with her students to India, Peru, and Tanzania through World Challenge as a Teacher Leader. Dr. Collins served as the lead instructional designer in 2021 for an online course for K–12 teachers hosted by the U.S. State Department, "STEM Innovations and Global Competence."

Katherine Counterman is the library media specialist at David and Terri Youngblood Elementary School in Katy, Texas, USA. She holds a master of library and information science (MLIS) degree from the University of Houston—Clear Lake and a master of education in reading from Bowling Green State University in Ohio. Besides being certified to teach library K–12, she holds certifications for teaching Pre-K–4 and as a K–12 reading specialist, as well as an English language learner supplemental. Her professional interests include the impact of graphic novels in educational settings and effective collaboration between the school library and other school departments. Katherine was named her campus' Teacher of the Year in 2017 while serving as the librarian, as well as Katy Independent School District's District-Wide Elementary Library Media Specialist of the Year in 2021. She has published in Booklist's Guide to Graphic Novels in Libraries and been featured in the Texas Library Association's podcast, *Libraries Transform Texas*. She is active in the Texas Library Association and has served on multiple committees, including as both a member and chair of the Little Maverick Graphic Novel Reading List.

Ashley B. Crane is an assistant professor and research and instruction librarian at Sam Houston State University, where she works to instill lifelong information literacy and library research skills in preservice and in-service educators. She began her career as a K–12 educator and has experience in school, public, and academic libraries. An ISTE-Certified Educator, Ashley's research interests include effective information literacy instruction and active learning.

Lesley Farmer is a professor at California State University (CSU). Long Beach, and she coordinates the Teacher Librarianship program. She also manages the CSU Information and Communication Technology Literacy Project. She earned her Master of Library Science degree at the University of North Carolina—Chapel Hill and received her PhD in adult education from Temple University. A frequent presenter and writer for the profession, she is a Fulbright scholar and has garnered several honors EdD from local to international groups. Farmer's research interests include school librarianship, digital citizenship, information and media literacy, and data analytics. Her most recent books are *Fake News in Context* (2021, Routledge) and *Reference and Information Sources and Services for Children and Young Adults* (2022, Rowman & Littlefield).

Eleanor Layo Freed is an expert in information and interactive experience design and literacy development in government, industry, and education. Layo holds an MLIS from San Jose State University, a bachelor's degree in fine art with a concentration in computer science from the University of California at Berkeley, and a master's degree in interdisciplinary social, cultural, and behavioral communication health. She also holds Collaborative Institutional Training Initiative research certifications, including work with children. Her research interests include copyright, cultural sustainability, ethical AI training practices, and playful youth-bound approaches to inspire full participation. Layo has published in *Public Services Quarterly*. She is a research member of the International Research Society for Children's Literature.

Deborah Lang Froggatt served as director of library services for Boston Public Schools for eight years. Prior to that, she directed the Boston Arts Academy/ Fenway High School Library. Her school library career and public school advocacy span twenty-six years. She also served in Danvers and Beverly, Mass., and in Brookfield, Ridgefield, and Woodbury, Conn. She was the Sherman, Conn., Library Director, and the Calumet Public Hospital (Michigan) Librarian. Academic credentials include: Miami University—BA, History; Princeton Theological Seminary—MA, Education; Southern Connecticut State University—MLS; Simmons University—PhD. Research focuses include the *informationally underserved* and school librarian assessment.

Neil Grimes serves as the subject librarian for the Department of Educational Leadership and Professional Studies and the Department of Teacher Education: Pre-K–12 at William Paterson University. He has nine years of experience as a school librarian working in a high school setting and has a total of thirteen years of experience working in K–12 urban education settings, serving in different educational roles, including as an elementary STEM teacher as well as a middle and high school social studies teacher. Neil holds an Master's in Library Science from Clarion University (now PennWest Clarion), an Master's in Education with a focus on Instructional Technology from Wilkes University, and is currently a doctoral student at Rutgers University in the School of Communication and Information. School Library Media Specialist PK-12, Social Studies 7-12 and Instructional Technology Specialist PK-12 certifications. His research interests include the digital divide, digital equity, libraries and wellness, educational technologies, emerging technologies, micro-credentials, school-university partnerships, organizational partnerships, college and career readiness, professional development, Google Slides and Bitmojis, academic library literacy programming, Real Men Read, literacy, read-alouds, and male mentorship. He has been published in *College & Undergraduate Libraries, Public Library Quarterly*, and *Knowledge Quest*. In addition, Neil has authored or coauthored four book chapters on topics ranging from how libraries support the mental health and wellness needs of communities to using Bitmoji and Google Classroom to support remote literacy instruction in high-needs schools to academic and school library partnerships: an organization-led collaboration in educational technology and the Pre-K–12 environment: implications for school leaders, teachers, and students. He also previously served as the cochair of the New Jersey Library Association's Professional Development Committee and currently serves as a committee member on the American Library Association's EBSS Curriculum Materials Committee, in addition to a few other library committees.

Elizabeth A. Gross is associate professor of Library Science and Technology at Sam Houston State University. She has a bachelor of arts in History and German from Northern Michigan University, an MLS, and a PhD in Learning Design and Technology from Wayne State University. Elizabeth was a post-doctoral fellow (mechanical engineering) at Kettering University. Her research interests include information needs of master's students and early career school librarians, graduate engineering students, perceptions of school librarianship, social justice in the school library, and artificial intelligence as a tool for librarians and library users. She is a member of the Texas Library Association, where she served as the Innovation and Technology Round Table chair; the Texas Computers in Education Association; the International Association of School Librarians; and the American Society for Engineering Education.

Amanda Harrison is an assistant professor at the University of Central Missouri in the Educational Technology and Library Science department. Previously, she worked for fourteen years as a school librarian in Illinois, Missouri, and Kansas in all grades, Pre-K–12. She holds a master's degree in social sciences from the University of Chicago, a master's in Teaching from Dominican University, and a master's and PhD in Library Science from Emporia State University. Her interests include school libraries and cross-cultural librarianship with a focus on issues of diversity, social justice, and access.

Gary Marks holds bachelor of arts degrees in history and political science as well as a master's degree in public policy and international affairs, all from William Paterson University. Gary earned his MLIS from Rutgers University and is a PhD candidate at Walden University. He currently serves as the reference and outreach librarian for the David & Lorraine Cheng Library, forging partnerships around campus and throughout the community to promote the library's value and resources. Gary also serves as an adjunct faculty member in William

Paterson University's Department of Political Science, teaching courses on American government, state government, and law in everyday life. He is the president of the Association of College and Research Libraries—New Jersey Chapter/College and University Section of the New Jersey Library Association, and has previously served as the vice president and legislative representative.

Rachel Anne Mencke is a graduate of the University of Chicago, where she studied Egyptian Archaeology, and the Graduate School of Library and Information Science at the University of Illinois at Urbana-Champaign. She began her career as a youth services librarian in Illinois public libraries before moving to the Kingdom of Bahrain to run the library of a bilingual K–12 school in Manama. Since 2014, Rachel Anne has been a school librarian at an independent Pre-K–8 grade school in Pacific Palisades, California, USA. She is an alumna of the American Library Association's International Library Networking Program and is currently serving on the ALA DEI committee and on the 2025 Caldecott Award Selection Committee.

Mary H. Moen is an assistant professor and coordinator of the School Library Media program at the Graduate School of Library and Information Studies at the University of Rhode Island. She has taught courses in information literacy instruction, school library services, media literacy, and materials and services for young adults. She is a former high school librarian and is currently president of her state association, School Librarians of Rhode Island. Her research interests include professional learning, media and digital literacy, and school library trends. She has published in *School Libraries Worldwide* and the *Journal of Research on Technology in Education*. She received her bachelor of arts from Brown University, and both her MLIS and PhD in Education from the University of Rhode Island.

Olga Polites taught high school English in South New Jersey from 1982 to 2022, and since 1999, has taught college composition at Rowan University in Glassboro, New Jersey, USA.. She has published in *The Philadelphia Inquirer*, *Newsweek, English Journal*, and *smerconish.com*. Since 2021, Olga has been the New Jersey chapter leader of Media Literacy Now, a nonprofit organization dedicated to ensuring all K–12 students are taught media literacy skills so that they become confident and competent media consumers and creators.

Chris Sperry is the director of curriculum and staff development for Project Look Sharp, a media literacy initiative at Ithaca College that he cofounded with Cyndy Scheibe in 1996. He taught secondary social studies, English, and media studies, and was an instructional coach for over forty years in Ithaca, New York, USA. He is the coauthor and producer of over 800 published lessons that integrate media decoding and critical thinking into the curriculum. He has delivered hundreds of Personality Development workshops for teachers and librarians around the world. He is the recipient of the 2005 PTA *Leaders in Learning Award for Media Literacy* and the 2008 NCSS *Award for Global Understanding*. He is the coauthor of the 2022 book *Teaching Students to Decode the World: Media Literacy and Critical Thinking Across the Curriculum*. Chris is the current director of a national initiative in partnership with AASL and NAMLE: Librarians as Leaders for Media Literacy *or* ML3.

Tricina Strong-Beebe is currently a K–8 school library media specialist in Burlington County, New Jersey, USA, and serves as a part-time professor for PennWest-Clarion University. Tricina serves as the advocacy chair for the New Jersey Association of School Librarians (NJASL) and brings almost twenty years of experience to the profession. This experience includes K–12 collegiate and public librarianship work. Tricina has presented at state, national, and international levels and has been published in a variety of publications. Her work has been recognized with the KARMA Foundation Scholarship, the Conover-Wihtol Scholarship, the Harriet DiLeonardo Active Teacher Grant, and Mark Schonwetter Holocaust Education Foundation. Tricina was awarded the 2021 New Jersey Association of School Librarians President's Award. She earned her MLS from PennWest-Clarion and holds additional graduate certification in teacher education and K–12 Maker Education from Rutgers University, New Brunswick, New Jersey, USA.

Steve Tetreault is the school library media specialist at the William R. Satz Middle School. He has been a front-line educator since 1998. He earned a master's in education and a PhD in educational administration and supervision, in 2006 and 2014, respectively, from the Rutgers University Graduate School of Education, as well as a master's of information degree in LIS (2019) from the Rutgers University School of Communication and Information. After more than twenty years as an English/language arts teacher for grades 7–12, Steve created and taught a required information literacy class for his school's seventh-graders for two years before transitioning into a school library position. Since 2018, Steve has contributed monthly to AASL's *Knowledge Quest* site and has written for *School Library Connection, Publisher's Weekly, American Libraries*, and other publications. He created SchoolLibrarianLearningNetwork.org, a curated site of free learning opportunities and resources of interest to school librarians. His most recent effort to contribute to the school library space is the *SLLN Podcast*, where school librarians share a lesson they teach so others can learn from their experiences. Since 2018, Steve has been a board member of NJASL. He firmly believes that the school library has become the last and best place for students to engage in authentic learning that will stay with them and help propel them to become lifelong learners. Therefore, school libraries staffed by qualified school librarians must be a priority for every school.

Beth Thomas has been a middle school librarian for over twenty years in Summit, New Jersey, USA. She holds an MLIS from Rutgers University and a bachelor of arts in English from Drew University. Beth has published in *School Library Connection, NJEA Review, Educational Viewpoints,* and *KQ*. She is a past president of NJASL and is currently a member of NJASL's advocacy team.

Holly A. Weimar is a library science professor and chair of the Department of Library Science and Technology. She holds an EdD in curriculum and instruction with an emphasis on teacher education from the University of Houston, an MLS from Sam Houston State University, and a bachelor of science in elementary education with a minor in mathematics from Stephen F. Austin State University. She has been a field experience coordinator and supervisor for school librarian practicum students and interns for more than a decade. Her research interests include artificial intelligence in the school library, advocacy for school librarians and the school library, information literacy, and school librarian knowledge and skills.